MW00653364

NOTHING HIGHER

NOTHING HIGHER

Why You Need to Descend in Order to Soar

Sunday Faronbi

Published in the United State of America by Rehoboth Consulting, Inc. This title may be purchased in bulk for educational, business, fund-raising, or sales promotional use. For information or requests to the Publisher for permission please e-mail NothingHigher@rehobconsulting.com.

Limit of Liability/Disclaimer of Warranty:
The views expressed in this work are solely those of the author. While the publisher and author have used their best efforts in preparing this book, they make no representations or warranties with respect to the accuracy or completeness of the contents of this book and specifically disclaim any implied warranties of merchantability or fitness for a particular purpose. No warranty may be created or extended by sales representatives or written sales materials. The advice and strategies contained herein may not be suitable for your situation. You should consult with a professional where appropriate. Neither the publisher nor author shall be liable for any loss of profit or any other commercial damages, including but not limited to special, incidental, consequential, or other damages.

By changing names and references, care has been taken to ensure that contributors' stories and anecdotes do not reflect poorly on anyone living or dead. Any resemblance to actual persons, living or dead, is purely coincidental. Neither the author nor the publisher assumes liability for the veracity of the information from contributors and those obtained through public sources such as newspaper reports, editorials, television, social media and others form of mass media.

Library of Congress Cataloging-in-Publication Data:
Name: Faronbi, Sunday M. - author.
Title: Nothing Higher - Why You Need to Descend in Order to Soar / Sunday Faronbi.
Description: Omaha, Nebraska: Rehoboth Consulting, Inc., [2021]
Subjects: Humility | Personal Transformation | Business Motivation | Leadership
Library of Congress Control Number: 2021908662
Includes bibliographical references and index.

Identifiers:
978-1-7371459-0-5 (paperback) | ISBN
978-1-7371459-2-9 (hardback) | ISBN
978-1-7371459-1-2 (eBook) | ISBN

Cover concept: Kristy Grindstaff
Cover design: Petercover

Due to the dynamic nature of the internet, any web addresses or links contained in this book may have changed since publication and may no longer be valid.

For Juliana, Paul, Matthew, Daniel, and Esther;
the five people that are being used daily
to teach me the value of humility.

CONTENTS

ACKNOWLEDGMENTS

A project like this could not have been undertaken successfully without the help and active involvement of many people. In my research for this book, I reached out to many friends, family members, colleagues, associates, and mentors. The level of response I received was unbelievable. As a result of their contributions, you will find in this book the collective wisdom and insight of many people on the subject of humility.

First, my special thanks go to internationally acclaimed speaker and author of the best-selling book *Natural Born Winners*, Robin Sieger, for planting the seed in me about making this book stand by itself. I also appreciate his willingness to write the foreword.

Additionally, I'm grateful to the leaders who spent a portion of their valuable time to sit with me to discuss and respond to the many questions I posed to them. They even shared some things I didn't know to ask! The insight and experiences they shared are invaluable. With much respect, I'm personally indebted to Gary Hoyt, former Lead Pastor at Bellevue Christian Center (BCC) in Bellevue, Nebraska. The same goes for Walter Hooker, Senior Associate Pastor at BCC. Also included on this short list is my dear friend and brother Femi Awodele – author, speaker, and Executive Director at Christian Couples Fellowship International. Each of these men invested and poured into me. Their wisdom and insights have been indispensable in making this a successful project for me to undertake. I'm eternally grateful to them.

Furthermore, I appreciate the contributions of the following people who shared their perspectives, experiences, and stories by responding to numerous weekly surveys over a period of several months between October 2017 and July 2018. They tirelessly responded to my questions each week and offered valuable insights. You will see their first names sprinkled throughout the pages of this book whenever appropriate. These contributors are: Adekunle Ayoade, Banke Adebowale, Bob McCoy, Brenda Kucera, César Hernandez, Deborah Joy, Hope Valentine, Jacqueline Schnider, Katherine Fox, Kevin Barrett, Kimberly Powers, Kolawole Jinad-Akande, Kristy Grindstaff, Mary Birchenough, Mary Coleman, Mel Kaup, Melba Hooker, Nair Hernandez, Nike Douglas, Olu-Samuel Akintobi, Olumuyiwa Olofinjana, Omolara Akinbola, Raquel Porter, Rebecca Fegan, Remi Odediran, Richard James, Temitope Olalude, Vivien Obieke, and Yemmy Adeyemi-Ojo. Some of these individuals also gave me the occasional push I needed to get this book finished. I'm gratified by their gentle pushing and prodding.

Moreover, I'm thankful to a core group of close friends and family members who agreed to review the finished manuscript prior to publication. Their wisdom and insight provided me with both the encouragement I sought and the critical feedback I needed. I've already named some of the people in this group. One person yet to be named is my longtime friend and brother Dr. Kayode Soladoye of Pensacola, Florida.

In addition, I must acknowledge the important work done by my very good friend and former colleague, Kristy Grindstaff who came up with the design concept for the cover of this book. She worked tirelessly and spent countless hours to meet my sometimes-impossible demands on quality and modifications. Yet, she happily delivered each time with delight, grace and enthusiasm.

I cannot forget to acknowledge a powerful group of family and friends who lend their voices to the body quotes in the text of this book during the narration of the audiobook version. These people with strong, angelic voices include Bob McCoy, Evell Thomas, Hope Valentine, Jean Duffy, Matthew Faronbi, Peggy Dunston, and Richard Nakai. In addition, Bob McCoy used his professional voice for the opening and closing credits of the audiobook. Thank you for allowing your voices to be heard around the world in support of this work.

I'm also thankful to members of my immediate family who

Acknowledgements

have been an invaluable source of encouragement during this process over the almost seven years it has taken to get this book completed and published. Doing life with them daily taught me a lot about this subject.

I am so grateful to have been blessed with such an amazing circle of family, friends, mentors, and associates who felt their time investment in me and this project was worth the effort.

Finally, I give glory to God for the grace and wisdom He gives me daily to do what I'm able to do. There's no way this is possible without Him. I'm grateful for the privilege I have, to draw strength from Him in order to accomplish all I've been called to do.

PROLOGUE

It was a bright Friday morning in August. After the overnight rain showers, the sun was finally peeking out from behind the clouds. As I walked up the stairs of the Kuala Lumpur Convention Centre in Malaysia, I noticed that while it was quiet outside, the inside of the convention center was a hub of activity.

On reaching the second floor, I walked toward the upscale coffee shop in which my meeting was supposed to be taking place. Once I passed through the opening that broke through the see-through, makeshift fence that cordoned the coffee shop from the rest of the wide-open corridors of the center, he saw me. He was talking to someone but quickly concluded the conversation.

He walked toward me; his right hand stretched out.

"Good morning. How are you?" he said in a barely noticeable Scottish accent.

I shook his hand. "I'm fine. How about you?"

"I'm good. Please have a seat."

This was Robin Sieger, the internationally-acclaimed speaker and bestselling author of the book *Natural Born Winners*, sold in over ninety countries, translated into twenty languages, and turned into a number-one-rated television series. Two days earlier, I was in the audience of more than three thousand Toastmasters, listening to him deliver a powerful motivational message. He was the keynote speaker during the opening ceremonies of Toastmasters International's first annual convention held outside of North America. But now, he was talking to me. I had approached him the previous day to request a private discussion and he obliged, suggesting that we meet in the coffee shop.

After we had talked for a while, I asked about his experiences as an author and a speaker. As he spoke, our discussion led me to tell him about a book I had just started writing at that time. He asked me what the book was about, and I told him it was about selfless leadership, highlighting the three major sections. One of those sections was on humility. His next comment surprised me. He asked, "Why don't you write a book about humility in leadership?"

As I thought about that question over the next several days, I began to realize how important this could be, so I put my planned book on hold to take on the challenge Mr. Sieger had just proposed. That's how my journey into writing this book began. Once I started, I increasingly saw how important humility is for anyone, and not just for those in leadership positions.

One picture that emerged for me as I started to ponder the topic of humility was a discovery that people who are truly humble consider others better than themselves. I found out that a lot of us struggle with this idea. We might look at someone and subconsciously feel, "I'll say the right words. I'll use the right language. I'll even compliment them and tell them how much better they are than me in this particular area (whatever that is). But I know in my mind that I'm truly better than they are."

Most people fall into this trap all the time. We don't plan to; we just do. I know that I do. It's probably not conscious for many of us. It just happens. And because it's unconscious, our behavior will also reflect it if we don't pay attention.

What do I mean when I said those who are truly humble consider others better than themselves? Does it mean that I should feel inferior to others? Not at all! Does it mean that I should make myself a doormat for others to trample upon? Far from it!

These types of questions come up because oftentimes, humility is seen as a sign of weakness by many. This is a common misconception. A selfless and humble person should not be mistaken for a weak one. In fact, there is an incredible amount of courage and strength involved in practicing humility in the ways that I describe in this book. Unfortunately, this sort of courage isn't always rewarded, especially within teams or in organizations. I am convinced that those who excel at self-promotion and self-praise are often the ones who get promoted to leadership positions, and many of them end up failing miserably in those positions. I believe this explains why effective leadership continues to elude many organizations today.

With the way humility is perceived, why would anyone want to be humble? What's the value in being humble? Everything in our culture exalts the exact opposite. Pride and ego are the order of the day. Humility is abased at every turn. We continue to learn to be selfish, as long as it leads to the fulfilment of our self-serving goals. It's much easier for me to choose my best interests than it is for me to choose yours. We are encouraged to pursue what makes us happy. It's all about me – what makes *me* better; what makes *me* look good; what makes *me* get ahead; what makes *me* more money; what gives *me* more esteem; what gives *me* a richer, fuller life.

However, real humility means choosing unselfishness over my best interests. This choice could mean different things to different people. For me, that includes considering others' interests when they don't go against my values. A good friend told me that humility is "putting others' needs in front of yours."[1] Another friend thinks humility is having "a heart that seeks to elevate and serve others before self."[2] Temitope, who is an economist, sees it as "putting other people into consideration rather than one's selfish interests."[3] Rick Warren said, "True humility is not thinking less of yourself; it is thinking of yourself less."

Being humble involves making a conscious effort to choose other people's needs and interests over your own. Another dear friend and colleague told me that it is "being able to put your selfish desires aside in order to make a positive difference for someone else."[4] And yet another associate understands it as "reaching out to the needy at the expense of one's own comfort."[5]

We can go on and on about the many traits found in people who are humble. One thing that is certain is that it can show itself in different ways through different people across diverse cultures and backgrounds. But one other important attribute of humility is confidence. A genuinely humble person can be confident without being arrogant or cocky. You can respect other people and choose their needs over yours while at the same time maintaining your self-respect and having a high level of self-regard for who you are. In fact, I think having a healthy dose of self-regard is important to being humble because you know who you are. With self-regard, you understand and accept your own strengths and weaknesses. You appreciate who you are and understand who you are not. Mother Teresa once said, "If you are humble nothing will touch you, neither praise nor disgrace, because you know what you are."

Writing in a *New York Times* blog post in November 2013, Tony Schwartz proposed that "genuine humility is a reflection of neither weakness nor insecurity. Instead, it implies a respectful appreciation of the strengths of others, a lack of personal pretension and a more relaxed sense of confidence that doesn't require external recognition."[6] With humility, you can celebrate others for being strong in the areas that you are weak. At the same time, you don't look down on them for being weak in the areas of your strength. Someone wrote to tell me that humility is "coming to terms with my rightful place in God's creation – neither elevated nor debased, but a full recipient of His grace. It is recognizing that the gifts He has placed in my life are just that: gifts."[7] If you see your natural talents and strengths as gifts, you are humbled for being a recipient of such gifts that you have not earned.

In the first chapter of this book, we will start off by defining humility from different perspectives. Even though humility can be approached from multiple angles by diverse peoples and cultures, we will see a coherent picture emerge about what it is. In chapter two, we will look at why humility is important for each one of us individually. We will explore the benefits that come from being humble. From chapters three to seven, I take a look at five major areas through which I think humility can be learned and is expressed: through gratitude, in expressions, with respect, through knowledge, and in receiving. This list is by no means exhaustive, and I'm sure you can think of a few more ways in which we can be humble.

All around us are ways we can learn the essence, value, and rewards of being humble. It is my hope that with this book, you will recognize the importance of cultivating and developing the traits and skills that lead to true humility.

FOREWORD

In my late twenties, I was diagnosed with cancer and spent six days in the hospital awaiting the outcome of radical surgery. I spent much of that time obsessing about death – *my* death. My mood swings were considerable – one moment I was fully confident in making a full recovery; the next, I'd be inconsolably distressed about missing the eulogy at my own funeral.

Facing one's (apparently imminent) mortality is a sobering experience – it's very difficult to predict how you will respond to those circumstances. Inevitably, you will reflect on the life you have lived, on the loves you may have lost, on the opportunities you may have squandered, and the personal issues you've left unresolved. More positively, you will take comfort in your successes and great accomplishments.

During that time of reflection, I wondered how I wanted to be remembered. If there was space on my tombstone for only one word, what would it be? Should it be a word bringing to mind an academic or sporting accomplishment? Should it try to sum up all of my potential and how it was thwarted all too soon by this cruel disease? Or might it be a reflection on me at my most dashing: "Robin Sieger, skydiver"?

I was surprised at how quickly I dismissed all of those ideas. I was equally surprised at how quickly I settled on my single word. It was a word that made sense to me, a word that had visceral meaning. The single word that would appear on my tombstone was "humble." There was a problem though.

At 29 years of age, I was not a humble man. Carrying all of the conventional insecurities of early adulthood, I was too often boastful and conceited, smug in my own little world, imagining greater of myself than I am sure the world at large did.

I decided then and there that, if I recovered, I would become a humbler person. To do this I would need to find a role model whose example I could aspire to. Someone I knew personally, not some mythologized historical figure. I knew that it had to be Stephen.

Stephen had died just a year before. We had met at school and rapidly became the best of friends with laughter punctuating every conversation we ever had. At our school, classes were set according to ability, and so we were rarely in the same schoolroom together: my academics were modest; his were stellar. He had a brain the size of a planet and breezed through school with the highest marks in every subject, learning Russian "just for fun" in his final year. At Oxford University, he graduated with first class honors and was invited to stay to complete a doctorate. He represented his college on University Challenge (the cerebral British television quiz show for university students). Whether the question was on the arts, physics, or history, it was usually Stephen who would answer his team's questions.

I remember being with Stephen when we met a confident young fellow determined to demonstrate his knowledge of opera to a small group. He referred to an obscure piece by a well-known composer and sounded deeply knowledgeable to me. Stephen listened with interest, then added some details about the opera's origins and gently corrected one or two of the fellow's descriptive errors, passing his knowledge off simply as "something he read in an article recently." The fellow was on the back foot and it was clear to all that Stephen had the opportunity to deflate his pomposity. But he didn't – he didn't show off; he didn't belittle. In fact, he simply thanked the fellow for introducing such an interesting topic. He was simply humble, and with that quality comes kindness, compassion, and thoughtfulness.

Being humble is not fashionable, I admit. Today, we are drawn to fame, power, money, and status – these are the qualities that engender respect and admiration. Prized, single words for a tombstone these days would be "ruthless," "aggressive," and "driven." But while fashions come and go, values are enduring and of greater significance to the human condition than the much sought after "fifteen minutes of fame."

Foreword

Nothing Higher is a brave and lucid argument for a return to enduring values. This book explores the true nature of humility. Time and again, it demonstrates what a powerful and positive quality humility is – how it inspires, motivates and lifts us to go further and do better than we had imagined possible. It is a quality that I aspire to every day.

Robin Sieger
Crieff, Scotland
August 2020

CHAPTER 1
WHAT IS TRUE HUMILITY?

A man's gift makes room for him,
and brings him before great men.[1]

- King Solomon

T he story was told of a horse rider during the American Revolutionary War who came across a few soldiers trying to move a heavy log without success. The horse rider stopped and watched the soldiers' futile efforts to move the log for a few moments. Then he noticed a corporal, the leader of the team, just a few feet away from the soldiers. He was standing by, just watching as his men struggled.

The horse rider couldn't believe it. Finally, he asked the corporal why he wasn't helping the men, to which he replied, "I am the corporal. I give orders!"

Shocked at the corporal's response, the horse rider said nothing. He simply dismounted his horse, walked to the soldiers, and proceeded to help them lift the log. With his help, they were able to eventually complete the task.

Once the mission was accomplished, the horse rider quietly walked back to his horse and mounted it. As he rode off, he said to the corporal, "The next time your men need help, send for the commander in chief!"

Who was this kind, thoughtful, and helpful horse rider? George Washington, *the commander in chief.*

To me, this story illustrates one of the many unusual ways through which humility can reveal itself. Here, we see a leader who was willing to stoop low to help people who were several rungs of the ladder beneath him. Contrast this with the behavior of the corporal, who felt some aspects of the job were beneath him. Unfortunately, you will find the corporal's attitude in every stratum of personal and business relationships today.

Before we begin to look fully into the myriad of ways that humility is either present or absent in people, let's backtrack for a moment and take a closer look at what it is and where it comes from.

Humility comes from the Latin word *humilis*, which literally means "low." One dictionary definition of humility says it is "a modest or low view of one's own importance." Did you notice that it doesn't say that you're not important? In fact, it implies that you are important. What it conveys is that your view of your importance is low in your own eyes. During one of our discussions, Gary Hoyt, a great mentor and friend, told me that humility is "not the absence of any thoughts about self."[2] It doesn't mean that you're not thinking about yourself. But neither does it mean being completely self-absorbed. It connotes the idea of thinking about yourself in the right way. For each one of us, this right-thinking about oneself can express itself in different ways.

To Rick from Bellevue, Nebraska, humility is "thinking more of others than you think of yourself."[3] Walter, also of Bellevue, asserts that it's "not thinking less of yourself, but thinking of yourself less."[4] For me, I see it as simply having the correct view of your own importance when you think about yourself. Charles Spurgeon described humility as "to make a right estimate of one's self." In other words, it's all about the way you see yourself. It's about your own view of your importance. And the way you see yourself will definitely show up in each interaction you have with other people.

For starters, a humble state is the state of not thinking that you're better than other people. Remi sees humility as "an attribute of not thinking highly of yourself, not seeing yourself as being better than others, though you could have been favored on almost every side by divine providence."[5]

As already stated, your level of humility determines how you see yourself. How you see yourself will determine how you carry yourself. Ironically, how you carry yourself is what tells others whether or not you're humble. Kevin sees humility as the recognition that "you are no more important than any other person; it's putting others first."[6] My good friend, Nair from North Carolina, believes that you're humble "when your views about yourself – what you have achieved or what you possess – don't make you feel superior to anyone."[7] Someone with a humble spirit does not go around with a rarefied air of superiority just because of their accomplishments. Dr. Melba Hooker says you are seen as humble when you "consider others and their needs before your own."[8]

As you can see from these insights from people with different backgrounds, it is obvious that humility is communicated through our behaviors. Others see humility in you through your actions. It's not something you tell others that you have or possess; they infer it from their observations of your words and deeds. Can you imagine me telling you how humble I am? Depending on the context, the moment those words leave my mouth, the opposite is true. If you say you're humble, people can quickly see through that thin veil of false modesty to recognize your oversized ego. Humility is what others see in you because of their interactions with you; it is not something that you say you are.

A Gift Worth Giving
To most people, a gift is something that you offer someone without expecting anything in return. Usually, a gift is not owed; it is given. While it may not be cheap to the giver, it comes free to the person receiving it. Personally, I've always believed that what matters is not the value of the gift but the thought behind it. It is a communication of the fact that the giver is thinking about the recipient. It may have minimal or no monetary value, but could mean the whole world to the person on the receiving end. It could be priceless to the beneficiary.

Have you ever received a gift? Many of us have, and receiving a gift is usually accompanied by some of the most positive feelings and emotions you could ever imagine. As a husband and father, I love to see the reactions from my wife and children when I give them something they have longed for. It's priceless! Sometimes, the reaction is similar even when they have neither desired nor expected the gift. A pleasant surprise!

That's the way I see humility – a pleasant surprise gift that we can spring on other people unsuspectingly. It's a surprise because they're usually not expecting it, and it's a gift because of the emotions that it evokes.

Have you ever thought of humility as a gift? I think it is. I think it's a gift that we give to those we come into contact with. It's a gift that transcends most gifts. It's a gift whose value and importance can only be determined by its beneficiary. It's a gift that opens the heart of the receiver to the giver. It's a gift that will create opportunities and open doors for you. It's a gift that will make room for you.

Inherited or Learned

Some say that a few are born humble, while most of us must learn humility. I'm not sure that anyone can truly claim humility as a genetic trait. What I do believe is that the environment in which we grow up shapes our beliefs and character. I think humility is one of those things that you *Humility is a gift that* unintentionally pick up from your *transcends other gifts.* surroundings, especially at an early age. Moses, who led the Jews out of slavery from Egypt, is a good example of this. I'll share more about him later in the book.

Since I knew very little about American history until much later into adulthood (after I had relocated to the United States), my first contact with Benjamin Franklin was through the pages of science books while I was in high school. Most Americans know him as one of the founding fathers of the United States of America, but he was also one of the great inventors of the eighteenth century. In his autobiography, he described several incidents in

What is True Humility?

which his *vanity* (as he referred to pride) reared its ugly head, and how he learned lessons in humility. This approach to picking up the traits of humility is true for many of us. In our formative years, we either learn humility from what we observe or we learn it from the things we suffer. Sometimes, the lessons of humility from our sufferings come much later in life.

It reminds me of the story I heard some time ago about a man who received a promotion to the position of vice president of the company he worked for. The promotion got into his head, and for several weeks, he boasted to anyone who cared to listen that he was now a VP. His bragging came to a sudden end one day when his wife, so embarrassed by his behavior, said, "Listen, Bob, it's not that big of a deal. These days everyone's a vice president. They even have a vice president of peas down at the supermarket!" With his bubble busted, a deflated Bob called the local supermarket on the phone to find out if this was true. "Can I speak to the vice president of peas please?" he asked, to which came the reply, "Which one? Of fresh or frozen?" It seemed that there was not just one vice president of peas in that supermarket. There were two of them! It confirmed what his wife had said: "These days, everyone's a vice president!" Bob learned a vital lesson about humility that day. Just as humility can be learned in our formative years, it can also be learned as adults.

While maturity, experience, and the unwanted consequences of our prideful behaviors can steer us towards humility, it can also be more difficult to become humble as we get older. This is because we first must unlearn whatever egocentric tendencies or behaviors we have already picked up. Yes, it may be difficult, but it can be done. My intent in this book is to show you how. Your success in life may depend on it. Much will depend on how badly you want it or how valuable you think it is. I also intend to show you how valuable it can be to you. There's a Zulu proverb that says, "Plenty sits still. Hunger is a wanderer." Are you hungry? Do you truly want to do more and achieve more? Do you want to develop better relationships with those you encounter? Do you aspire to soar and ascend to greater heights – greater things? If your response to any of these questions is yes, then I invite you to come on this journey with me; we'll explore together.

NOTHING HIGHER

At the end of each of the remaining chapters, I've included a "What You Can Do" section that contains practical tips and techniques. Many of these are very simple steps that anyone can follow. I encourage you to practice them regularly, no matter how uncomfortable they may be for you at the beginning. When you stay with these tips and do not quit, those new behaviors will soon turn into habits that you will come to appreciate and value.

It is equally important to explore the reasons every person must seek to be humble, so the next chapter starts off by taking a closer look at why humility is important.

When you practice the principles in this book and grow in humility, you will begin to see new worlds revealed to you. Doors that were previously slammed shut are likely to swing open. A wide range of opportunities will appear. That's because being humble – the state of having a low view of one's own importance – is a gift. It's a gift that will make room for you. It's a gift that will bring you before great people.

There is nothing higher.

CHAPTER 2
WHY YOU NEED IT

The mind is not a vessel to be filled,
but a fire to be kindled.

- Plutarch

My daughter is one of the most inquisitive people I know. From the moment she could talk, she was always asking questions. And her questions ranged from the routine and mundane ones that most toddlers ask to the deep and profound ones that I had no answers for. Most of these, as you may have guessed, began with "why." While I was able to provide logical responses to many of her questions, there were some that simply stumped me. I especially remember the ones that I had difficulties explaining to a three-year-old.

"Daddy, why is the sky blue?"

"Why is water wet?"

I just had no answers for them at the time. How do you respond to "Why is water wet?" Sometimes, to avoid giving an answer, I would divert her attention to something else to cover up my ignorance on the subject. That worked when she was little. As she got older, she must have realized that her dad was not as smart as she had thought. Now, as a teenager about to start college (at the time of this writing), she turns to Google to answer her questions!

Asking why prior to undertaking anything is a natural question for many of us. Just as it was with my daughter, many of us start asking why very early in life. Our curiosity gets the best of us every time. A knock on the door piques the interest of everyone inside the house. When that happens, most people would stop what they're doing until they find out who's at the door. The chime or ding from your smart phone draws your attention to it, and you immediately want to find out what just happened in the tangled World Wide Web! Even for those of you who are disciplined enough not to allow those pocket-sized computers rule your lives, often something keeps nagging at you until you find out the reason for the sound that just came from your phone. It's like an itch that you just have to scratch!

Writing in a *Psychology Today* blog post, Dr. Mario Livio, an astrophysicist and the author of *Why? What Makes Us Curious*, said that "when we encounter phenomena that appear to be incompatible with our previous knowledge or when we feel that there is a gap created by uncertainty, we are driven to seek new insights that will reduce the unpleasant sensation."[1] In layman's terms, Dr. Livio is saying that we're curious because we want to understand something better, which is probably the reason you're reading this book. And you may be wondering and asking yourself, Why humility? It is therefore a good idea for us to start by exploring why humility is important.

Why be humble? What benefits does humility bring you? Or to anyone for that matter?

Not for the Faint of Heart
To begin, I've found out that there are quite a number of people who see humility as a weakness. Many confuse being humble with being docile, weak, or submissive at all times. For these people, the true value of humility is not appreciated. Walter Hooker, currently a pastor at Bellevue Christian Center, served for fifteen years in the United States Air Force. He told me that in most cases, the military "wants people who can take charge and always be in control. Sometimes, humility is not the answer to their situations. It's not as valued as taking charge. As a result, those who exhibit humility may not move along in their military careers as well as

those who seem to know it all and want to take charge and be in control."[2]

A similar situation is common in many organizations. Most businesses desire the visibly take-life-by-the-horns type of a leader. And many believe that the kind of leader who takes charge cannot be humble. They view these two as mutually exclusive. Pastor Hooker further told me that many of these kinds of leaders think some semblance of humility is "only needed when they've messed up."[2] If that's the case – if humility means being weak – why would anyone want to be humble?

On the contrary, most of the people I spoke to on this topic do not agree with this assertion that humility translates to being weak. The manner in which they described humility, along with the attributes they see in those they consider humble, spoke volumes about the courage and the inner strength that is essential in humility. Mary, who works in the compliance department of a big company in the financial services industry, spoke of humility as not being "a feigned effort, but a true knowing of oneself."[3] She further told me about the story of a family member that she considered humble but also very driven from an early age. "She had self-imposed goals such as deciding to never miss a day of school and to maintain academic excellence. That drive led her to eventually own her medical practice," she wrote. Would you say that's a description of someone who's weak? I don't think so!

Both Kimberly, an insurance adjuster, and Deborah, a project scheduler, spoke glowingly of their fathers as examples of people of great humility. Kimberly wrote about how her dad "spent nearly every waking hour quietly serving others."[4] Of her dad, Deborah observed, "My father was one of the most humble people I've known. Everything he did in his life was about serving other people."[5] To these people, the humility they observed in their fathers was an endearing trait to them. It drew them closer to their dads. They had better relationships as a result. Do you have relationships that need to improve? I'm sure you do! We all have relationships that can be

> *Humility is not a feigned effort, but a true knowing of oneself.*
>
> Mary Coleman

better. Humility can help you deepen connections with people you love. Being humble can translate to improved relationships.

I admit that some of these descriptions of what is seen as humility may not be that of a big deal to you. But let's remember that humility speaks to how others see us. It's not about how we see ourselves. And usually, no one knows us better than family members with whom we have spent most of our lives, so if these people see their relatives as being humble, then we can be sure that their testimony is true. This point is further driven home when you consider that there are countless others who can easily spot, in those closest to them, everything that humility is not. False humility can be seen very quickly, so we must truly and genuinely seek to be humble.

It's Not About Me

Brenda told me a shocking story involving someone she used to work with. I'll call him Roger. In Brenda's words:

> Our golden retriever had been very sick with a rare condition. It broke our hearts that we had to put our sweet Shilo to sleep on Valentine's Day about four years ago. Through my tears, I sent an email to my coworkers who would need to know that I was going to be out of the office (by taking a vacation day) on that February 14 day and why. Roger's reply was "Been there; done that. Make the most of it." I've never looked at Roger the same way since then. He has a way of listening and then twisting his reply so it's all about him. I knew then that Roger's way is to think first of Roger, before others.[6]

People who lack humility have a way of turning everything around so it's about them. That's what we see here with Roger. And we can see the results with the effects it had on Brenda. Some who exhibit this behavior do it under the pretext of false modesty. Many of those who behave this way may be doing it involuntarily, but the fallouts are nonetheless devastating simply because they communicate deception. As Jane Austen puts it, "Nothing is more deceitful than the appearance of humility." As a result, it is very important for us to be able to detect and identify situations where something else is being peddled as humility. Here are some traits of false humility:

Excessively Modest
Some may actually try to exhibit humility in such an extreme fashion that makes it look ugly. They try very hard to show humility, even though their hearts are not really in it. Their real intentions are to draw attention to themselves. But they don't want it to look that way, so they try to cover it up with overdone humility, which tends to backfire. Someone wrote to tell me that this display of "excessive 'hang time' seems to beg for more attention," to the extent that you want to yell, "This is pitiful. Stop it!"[7]

Your Praise is Mine
Then there are those who humbly and quietly accept praise for something they haven't done. You may have seen that before at your place of work. This type of behavior is really annoying to the people who actually deserve the recognition. A friend told me of a time when a former boss took credit for someone else's work. This boss "graciously, humbly, and publicly accepted praise and thanks for a project that my friend had completed" without any input or assistance from the boss. My friend concedes the fact that "when I work for someone else, they own my work products." However, she further stated, "Most other bosses that I know have always ensured some measure of credit went to the actual individual or team responsible for the success. I realized that this particular boss was insecure in her abilities and position, so I let it go. From then on, I knew her for who she was and managed to find a job in another department."[8]

This recognition-pilfering manager lost a valuable team member to another department because of her own insecurity.

Two-Faced
Some seem to have two different personas when it comes to humility. One is for the public – their audience or customers. This is usually the genial and humble side. Behind the scenes, however, the uglier personality emerges when dealing with those closest to

them. They bully and abuse the people who work with them. Someone wrote to tell me about a church worship leader who would say, "'All this is for Jesus' from the stage, but off the stage would yell at team members and musicians if they made mistakes."[9] As a result, those who knew this unpleasant side of this leader did not trust him to lead them in worship.

No Thanks Necessary

How about those who are constantly insisting on not being thanked? The giveaway here is the frequency with which they talk about not wanting to receive thanks. They refer to what they had done that was not acknowledged and end with the fact that they were not doing it for the recognition. A friend told me about one such individual who "continually brought up how much they don't need to be in the limelight or be thanked for what they do, yet brought it up nearly every time someone would listen." My friend feels empathy for those who behave this way because what it tells her is that they are "seeking significance and have not found it." [10]

> *Nothing is more deceitful than the appearance of humility.*
>
> Jane Austen

From all of these, you can see that traces of false humility can be easily detected. Just as *faux* humility doesn't deceive most people, being truly humble is also clearly seen. And it has a lot of upsides.

Why Humility is Important

There are many qualities that flow from being humble. Some of these include forgiveness, truthfulness, patience, generosity, kindness, respectfulness, compassion, self-confidence, inner strength, and many more. All of these are traits that will endear you to those you come into contact with. They make you irresistible. As a result, you find favor and receive goodwill in many areas of your life. They're like magnets that attract good things to you. Here are a few of them:

Peace Like No Other

I believe that one of the most enduring benefits of learning to be humble is the peace that it brings. Gone are all the internal struggles of wanting to outshine or outperform others. Gone are the burning desires of wanting to be better than others. To be clear, this doesn't mean that you are now devoid of ambitions and the desire to achieve success. Quite to the contrary! I strongly believe that the motivation to be accomplished and successful does not have to come from wanting to be better than others. Paul, an engineer who lives in Albuquerque, New Mexico, echoed this by writing me to say, "My dad works hard, is intelligent, and believes he can accomplish anything he puts his mind to. At the same time, he doesn't go to lengths to show all that he can accomplish or has accomplished. He is humble."[11]

Just as I Am
Similarly, being humble can help you accept yourself just as you are. When you quit comparing yourself to others, you silence the internal turmoil and the voices of self-doubt that seek to continually ask you whether you're enough – good enough, smart enough, fast enough, strong enough, pretty enough, or any of the other kinds of "enough" that you can conjure up in your mind. This type of negative self-talk does nothing other than weigh you down, thus preventing you from moving forward or achieving success.

There is a component of emotional intelligence called self-regard. It refers to respecting yourself while understanding and accepting your strengths and weaknesses. Self-regard is often associated with feelings of inner strength and self-confidence, no matter the undesirable traits you possess. In other words, you accept yourself for who you are, warts and all. Developing humility will help you with self-acceptance.

The motivation to accomplish does not have to come from wanting to be better than others.

Seeing Clearly
Once you begin to accept yourself for who you are, you also start to see yourself and others clearly. When you see yourself clearly, you are able to better understand your strengths and accept your limitations. As a result, you can clearly recognize the value that

others can add to you. As you embrace and leverage what others can do, you begin to achieve much more than what you can by yourself.

Having the Right Outlook

Seeing yourself clearly helps you to have the right outlook in life. When you see yourself with better clarity, you also begin to see things from much better and accurate viewpoints. You become more objective in your assessment of people and situations. This is what Kevin from Seattle, Washington, meant when he wrote to tell me that having humility "puts you into the proper mind perspective." As a coach and training consultant, he said that humility "helps you remember what is important in life – people, love, and caring for others."[12] When you recognize and remember what the real-life treasures are, you tend to be more grateful for what you have instead of focusing on what you don't have. It's a matter of having the right perspective.

Being Amenable

With humility, people see you as valuable and approachable. When you're seen as welcoming and agreeable, people will seek you out for the value you can add to them. Even if they don't seek you out, any advice that you offer will be received well because your humble disposition tells them that you have no ulterior motives. As Bob wrote to tell me, "If I have wisdom to offer, it makes that wisdom easier to receive."[13]

A Good Attraction

Being humble attracts trust and love from people. It also commands respect. Adekunle, a dear childhood friend who lives in Calgary, Canada, shared with me an example of this in the mayor of his city. [14]Mr. Mayor was humble, and he did not allow his leadership position to change the kind of person he was. As a result, he gained the trust, love, respect, and support of the people, which is

Humility helps you remember what is important in life.
Kevin Barrett

something rare with politicians. He won the hearts of the citizens of his city with his character. He was rewarded by being re-elected to continue in office for multiple terms.

An Effective Connector

When we exhibit humility, it helps us to overcome our own selfishness in order to communicate and connect effectively with others. Mary, an occupational therapist who lives in Honolulu, Hawaii, shared with me a humbling experience she had to go through. In her own words,

> My husband and I were in a pretty significant disagreement, and quite frankly, it was stressful. We were not seeing eye to eye at all but I felt a nudge in my heart that I needed to approach the situation with humility.
>
> I walked away from the situation for a few minutes, did some self-reflection, and prayed. It dawned on me that I needed to humble myself in that very moment, which I found extremely hard to do. I had to get rid of all the "but my husband isn't doing this or that" statements that were flooding my mind. I needed to truly humble myself and remove all the blame I had built up in my mind and assigned to him.
>
> A little later, I grudgingly approached him and shared a prayer I was going to begin saying every day. The prayer was not for God to change my spouse, but instead that He would change me. To be completely honest, it was not easy. But since that moment of humility, our marriage has become stronger, our days have become filled with happy moments, and we began to see eye to eye – a much better understanding of each other.[15]

Moments of humility such as the one described here help us get rid of our personal desires for selfishness and connect better with others. Mary added that this "allows far more riches than pride could ever deliver into our lives."

Something to Learn
It takes humility to learn from another person. To be teachable, you have to do away with whatever you think you already know and approach others with an inquisitive and open mind. Arrogant people usually come across as if they know it all and that no one can teach them anything. Here's a fact of life – no one person knows everything. I don't. Neither do you. Humility helps us to learn and grow from those that surround us.

Jacquie, from Calgary, Alberta, in Canada agrees. She said that being humble made her "realize that everyone has something to share. I might not know everything, but by being humble, I can learn as well as teach. By being humble, people are more apt to share with you. It draws people to you as opposed to turning them off."[16]

Engenders Respect, Favor, and Trust
Humility attracts to you a high level of admiration and esteem. You earn the respect of others and you're seen as trustworthy. I find a funny example of this in the story[17] that Sam from Aba, Nigeria, told me. This happened many years ago when he was working as an industrial and electronic instrumentation technician at a manufacturing facility. He had responded to a call that a machine on one of the production lines had stopped and needed repair.

On arrival, he exchanged pleasantries with the equipment operators, who knew him as someone they could trust because he had always dealt with them with humility. He asked them what the problem was with the machine. The leader of the group quickly pulled him aside and told him that the machine

Humility allows more riches than pride could ever deliver into our lives.
Mary Birchenough

was running too fast for them to catch up, so they pulled out a cable that made it stop. She pleaded with Sam that her team just needed a few moments to catch their breath before resuming production. Sam gave them the time they needed to rest, and then reinstalled the cable.

While I don't necessarily condone the dubious manner in

Why You Need It

which the operators went about getting a much-needed break (which I think says a lot about the operations leadership in the plant), I'm impressed that they were confident that Sam would not rat them out and report their treasonous behavior to higher-ups. They trusted him and gave him favor by telling him the truth right away.

Why did I call it favor? Because there were other technicians who attended to the problem before Sam was called, and they couldn't figure out the problem. They couldn't solve the problem because the operators did not tell them about the cable they had pulled out, so instead of Sam spinning his wheels and spending countless hours to troubleshoot a problem that was really nonexistent, he fixed it within a few moments. (Well, after giving them a thirty-minute break!)

> *Humility creates respect and makes integrity intact.*
> Olumuyiwa Olofinjana

Ego Check

Learning to be humble is a good way to continually check our ego at the door. With an unchecked ego, we can quickly become full of ourselves. Rick, who is self-employed wrote to me saying, "If we are not humble, we can become humbled by what happens to us."[18] He told me about the events surrounding his wife's sickness before she eventually passed away:

> When my wife was sick, I was having trouble getting the time needed to get work done. Some people that I knew, and others I didn't, started bringing food and donating money so that I could spend as much time with her as possible. At one point, we had more than twenty-five people who came from out of town to see her. All the food people had brought kept them fed so I wouldn't have to take the time to get that side of it figured out.
>
> I am someone that has always worked for what I have. When I couldn't, it was very humbling to

see what God can do when we get over ourselves
and let things happen and allow other people take
the lead away from you.

With the situation he found himself in, Rick learned to be
humble and to receive help when he most needed it. He learned to
check his ego.

Marital Bliss
When it comes to the importance of humility in interpersonal
relationships, the stakes are no higher than in the marriage
relationship. I'm no marriage expert, but after being married for
more than twenty-seven years, my own experience has shown me
that it takes constant doses of humility from either one or both
parties involved to make it work. If not, that marriage is headed
for the rocks. But don't take my words for it, let's ask an expert
on the matter.

Femi Awodele has been helping marriages recover from the
brink of collapse for about twenty years. As the executive director
of Christian Couples Fellowship International, he frequently
conducts marriage conferences around the globe and has spoken
on this topic to audiences in more than forty countries. Here's
what he told me about humility and marriage:

> In all my years of marriage ministry, I can say
> without any fear of contradiction that for many of
> the marriages I have dealt with, the ones that have
> ended up in divorce is primarily because of pride.
> I can prove in many different ways that pride or
> lack of humility is the reason for divorce. It may
> not be the original reason for the conflict, but the
> conflict eventually gets to a level where it
> becomes "Who is going to back down? Who is
> going to say I'm sorry?" This is where the
> problem lies!
>
> Humility is learning to say "I'm sorry," even
> when you believe you're right. One of the biggest
> issues in marriage is vulnerability. Most people

Why You Need It

don't want to be vulnerable, especially with their spouse. They think that if they're vulnerable, the other person will walk all over them, that they will take advantage of them. Humility is being vulnerable. Even for me personally, it took me a while to learn that. But once I did, I understood that this is the humility that God wants from me.[19]

All of the above show us why humility is a very important trait to be desired and cultivated for success in life. It is crucial in both personal and professional relationships.

For the Leader

As leaders, the rewards of humility become elevated for all of us. Before you begin to protest that you're not a leader, let me quickly remind you that you are. We're all leaders in one area or another of our lives. That's because, as John Maxwell puts it, "Leadership is influence; nothing more, nothing less." And we all have influence, whether we realize it or not. You have influence. So do I. Your sphere of influence may be different from mine. But there are people around you who are influenced and affected by what you say or do. In that respect, we are all leaders.

A pseudo leader always leaves you with a feeling of their greatness, while an authentic leader always leaves you with a feeling of your greatness.

As a result of our influences on others, many of these benefits of humility become extremely important for those who hold leadership positions in private and public organizations. According to a study by researchers from State University of New York and the University of Washington, humble people usually make the most effective leaders and are more likely to be high performers in both individual and team settings. Yes, you read that right – *humble people usually make the most effective leaders and are more likely to be high performers*! These researchers also found that workers who saw their managers as humble reported feeling more engaged at work and were less likely to quit their jobs. They concluded: "Overall, the meaning of expressed humility derived from our literature search and initial empirical testing appears to have important implications for employee attitudes and organizational outcomes in the workplace."[20] In other words, when leaders are humble, the effects are positive attitudes in the workplace and encouraging outcomes for the organization.

In another study, it was discovered that "when followers perceive humility in their leader, they will be more committed to the vision, more receptive of the leader's stated performance expectations and other vision implementation techniques, and more trusting that the leader's communication is genuine and thoughtful, compared with followers who do not perceive their leader as humble."[21]

I once heard someone say that executives are usually hired because of skills and experience but often fired due to their personality. This is not that difficult to decipher as you look at the reasons for many high-profile executive failures in recent history. The names that easily come to mind include Mike Jeffries (Abercrombie), Jeff Skilling (Enron), Thorstein Hein (Blackberry), and Joe Cassano (AIG). Many of these leadership failures have direct links to lapses connected to the absence of humility.

All I'm saying here is that the importance and benefits of humility cannot be overemphasized. Humility is the baseline for leadership. A leader without humility cannot truly lead. It's that simple. As a result, and with so many benefits too numerous to count, humility should be a highly desirable trait for every one of us. When anyone – whether or not they are in a recognized leadership position – lives his/her life from a solidly humble premise, he/she is naturally seen as being honest, trustworthy, and capable. These characteristics draw good things to them. That's the reason humility will help you soar to greater heights.

The good news is that even if these are not traits or abilities that come naturally for you, they can be learned. Starting with the next chapter of this book, we begin to look at ways that true humility can be developed.

Why You Need It

What You Can Do

As you read through the various reasons why humility is important in this chapter, what were the thoughts going through your mind? Did you see yourself in some of those examples? Which of the situations are specific to you? Did they trigger something in your mind?

I would like for you to create a list of how exhibiting humble traits can make a difference in your own life. Take a moment now to take stock of what being humble can do for you. You know yourself better than anyone else, right? So, take a look at your relationships – personal and professional – and outline where being humble will be beneficial to you. Make it personal. Make it real.

1. Think about an experience you had in which you could have shown humility but did not.

2. What were the reasons you behaved the way you did?

3. What benefits did you lose by behaving that way?

4. Describe what you could have done differently.

5. What were the benefits you would have received if you had behaved differently?

6. What could stop you from behaving this way in the future?

7. What can you do about it?

8. What will you do about it?

9. When will you do it?

10. To whom will you hold yourself accountable as you do it?

Now that we have a much better understanding of the benefits that being humble can confer on anyone, let's begin to look at how to develop it. We start with how appreciating others and the recognition of kind gestures can help.

CHAPTER 3
GRATITUDE IS KEY

We can only be said to be alive in those moments
when our hearts are conscious of our treasures.
- Thornton Wilder

Just a few decades ago, the sharing of folktales was common in many cultures. While you may not see much of it in the urban areas, I believe it is still happening today in many countries, cities, and villages. On most evenings as nightfall approaches, children sit in the rising glow of the moon listening intently to stories, usually told by an elderly person.

Growing up as a little boy in Africa, I had the privilege of hearing many genres of folktales. Even though I grew up in the suburbs of Lagos, which is a big city in Nigeria, I remember how on occasions, we would travel to my dad's village to visit with extended family members. Despite the fact that I was very young at the time, I can still remember sitting under a large tree with other kids listening to one of the adults tell us stories.

Often told in local, ethnic languages, these stories have a unique richness to them. In the Nigerian *Yoruba* culture, in which I was raised, animals tend to feature prominently in much of the folklore. These animals were often used as object lessons by excessively magnifying one or more natural attributes of the animals used in the stories. Here's one that I remember, and which

I later found out has several variations and parallels across many cultures around the world.

> The lion once got caught in a rocky cleft and could not get out. A horse came by, and the lion appealed to him, "Help me out of this cleft!"
>
> "I'll do that," answered the horse, "but you must promise not to eat me."
>
> The lion promised, and the horse dug with his hooves until he had freed the lion. However, as soon as the lion saw that he was free, he pounced on the horse and said, "Now I am going to eat you."
>
> "Really! Didn't you promise?" asked the horse. "Did we not agree that you would not eat me?"
>
> "That makes no difference now," shouted the lion. "But if you want to, we can go before a judge." The lion thought that as the king of the jungle, no animal would dare pass judgment against him.
>
> "Good," replied the horse. "But to whom shall we go?"
>
> "The fox," said the lion.
>
> The horse agreed to this, so they went to the fox, and the lion recounted what had happened.
>
> "Yes," answered the fox, "it seems to me that you must be right, Mr. Lion, but I cannot finalize my judgment until I have seen how the two of you were standing. I need to see the situation exactly as it played out."
>
> So, all three of them went to the rocky cleft, and the horse positioned himself in the same place he had stood. Then the fox told the lion to force himself back into the cleft. "Is that how you were standing?" he asked.

"This leg was a little more twisted," answered the lion.

"Then push yourself in a little more tightly. You must be in exactly the same position as you were when you asked the horse for help."

The lion pushed himself in a little more, and the fox asked again, "Is that exactly how you were standing?"

"This front leg was a little further inside."

"Then push yourself in, still a little more."

Finally, the lion had pushed himself in so tightly that he could not get out again.

"So," said the fox. "You are exactly where you were before. Now the horse can decide whether or not he's willing to help you get out again."

The horse, however, did not want to do so. Instead, he threw rocks at the lion until he was dead.

I still remember one of the main lessons from this story – being grateful and not repaying good deeds with evil. The story also highlights the perception of the fox as cunning and sneaky, and the lion as wanting to kill and eat anything that moves. Indeed, the fox was crafty, but the lion paid the ultimate price simply because of his refusal to show gratitude.

When someone does you a favor, the appropriate and expected response is to be thankful. It's the affirmation you give when things go your way. But there are some people who don't see this as a suitable response. Instead of being thankful, they try to take advantage of the good deed for their own selfish purposes, sometimes to the detriment of the party to whom they ought to be thankful. That was what the lion in this story tried to do, but the fox prevented that from happening.

While being thankful is good and should be encouraged, I

don't think it's the same as being *grateful*. In most cases, thankfulness results from specific actions that have been done for your benefit when things go your way because of the activities of another person. It's what happens when you're on the receiving end of a positive action from someone else. On the other hand, I believe that gratitude is an attitude – a way of life. It's how you respond, whether or not things turn out the way you expect. You respond that way because that's who you are, not just because of what was done for you or the good thing that you have received. You respond that way because you don't see what's been done for you as a right to which you have a claim.

Deservedly Mine
One of the major traits of most ungrateful people is a sense of entitlement. They seem to hold on very tightly to whatever comes their way. They can't let go. In their minds, they worked hard for it, after all. They deserved it! And since they deserve what they have, why be grateful? That's unnecessary! Right? The same goes for what anybody does for them. They expect to be the recipients of whatever comes to them. They're entitled. In fact, if the deed is not done well, or not done at all, they may become furious. Who are you to deny them of what is *appropriately* theirs?

Many people who live in Europe or North America are familiar with the TV show *Judge Judy*. I once saw an old episode of the show where this kind of entitlement played out in a ridiculous manner. The plaintiff had sued the defendant for not paying back a $2,000 loan. During the court session, there was a long dialogue between the defendant and Judge Judy.[1] As I watched the show, I paid close attention to the expressions on the faces of those sitting in that courtroom. Most of the people who saw this exchange were stunned by the defendant's attitude and her feeling of entitlement. It's likely you have also been shocked when you have experienced this same attitude.

The following are a few things that you will notice from the entitled person:

Huge Expectations
The entitled person has expectations that will seem irrational to

most people. They're entitled to your stuff just because you have more than they do. They are entitled to have you behave in a specific way towards them just because that's what seems right to them. It's all about them. You and your opinions don't matter. You owe them. Or someone else owes them. Or the government owes them. Somebody always owes them. That's the source of their entitlement.

I've seen several examples of this, especially with the social welfare program in many developed countries such as the United States, Canada, and some countries in Western Europe. Such welfare programs provide for and help people who are unable to take care of themselves as a result of temporary job loss, medical problems, or other situations beyond their control. While many are grateful for the government assistance in their times of need, I've seen examples of others who feel entitled, believing that the government owes them these services. As a result, their attitudes could be so off-putting sometimes that you want to slap some sense into them! Ralph Moody calls such people "dishonest." He said, "There are only two kinds of men in this world: honest and dishonest men. Any man who says the world owes him a living is dishonest."

The entitled person has expectations that will seem irrational to most people.

A friend once told me about one of his close relatives who felt that the government owed them health insurance and a monthly check. Arie (not her real name) had no marketable skills and worked earning minimum wage from a fast-food franchise. According to the report, Arie had multiple opportunities to improve herself and her situation. But she simply refused to try. As a result, she couldn't make enough money to take care of her own needs. She felt it was the government's responsibility to help her fill the gap. And she had an attitude about it.

My friend said he tried to reason with her. He told her that if everyone relied on the government this way, it would be a disaster because the government would not be able to cope. His words were, "I tried to tell her that an able-bodied person should take on the responsibility to earn their own way in life, that no one owes them anything. She flat out told me that she didn't see why she shouldn't be able to get money and health coverage from the government."[2]

This is what the world of an entitled person looks like. It's all about them and their needs. And their entitlement blinds them to how their behaviors come across to others. It breeds envy, greed, and restlessness. Instead of being grateful, they're thankless. Instead of being humble, they're prideful. They have a high view of their own importance. They think very highly of themselves and their needs, and every other person just needs to fall in line!

I've heard some people attribute this type of entitled behavior to immaturity. But I beg to differ. I don't think this has anything to do with age or level of maturity. It's simply the absence of humility. These behaviors have no age limits. Nor can they be ranked on a maturity scale. It's the same in the old and the young. It can be found in the juvenile and the mature. You are probably aware of the current general perception that millennials and the generations coming after them seem to be entitled. While I would not necessarily label entire generations as entitled, you do see instances that make you scratch your head with some of our younger friends. Kimberly recounted an experience she had interviewing an eighteen-year-old. Here's what she told me:

Any man who says the world owes him a living is dishonest.
Ralph Moody

> I was interviewing a prospective employee, and while discussing the pay, the applicant told me he could never work for only $14 per hour plus bonuses and an opportunity to work his way up to higher pay. He further said that he deserved at least $20 per hour and wasn't interested in starting at the bottom. This kid was only eighteen years old! He had never worked before, nor had he done any volunteer work! He came off to me as un-coachable and entitled. I still shake my head anytime I remember him.[3]

Gratitude Is Key

Most young job applicants are grateful for an opportunity to have a job, understanding that if they have no experience, they will most likely have to start at the bottom and learn. Many that are given such opportunity work hard, do their best, and know they can work their way up. This young man was not one of them. He had an attitude of entitlement and a very high view of his own importance. As a result, he passed on a good opportunity. I hope he's been able to learn from his mistakes.

Breeding the Entitled

For those of us who are parents or guardians, I believe we have an important responsibility to teach our children and wards how to be grateful for what they have. I think this is the best way to avert breeding the entitled. This is important because an entitled attitude is learned. It's something that we pick up from our surroundings, especially at a young age. If as a parent you strive to give your child every whimsical thing that they ask for, be careful. You may be raising an entitled child! I've had some parents tell me that they want to provide for their children things that they were denied when they were growing up. In an effort to do that, care should be taken to differentiate *needs* from *wants*. Even if you're able to give them all they can dream up, remember that you're not the only person who makes up their world. Eventually, they will grow up and leave the nest, and they will come across someone who will say no to something that they want. If this is the first time that they get that kind of response, how do you think they will react? Those reactions usually reveal the fruits that the entitled person produce. The fruits of entitlement include greed, bitterness, envy, resentment, and impatience. These will set up a young person for failure in life. This is the reason I love one mom's approach to her children's requests. Here's what she said:

> ... *an able-bodied person should take on the responsibility to earn their own way in life. No one owes them anything.*
>
> Rick James

My teenage children have expressed on a number of occasions they think it's unfair that I don't

39

provide them both with smartphones "like all their friends." I told them that when I was a teenager, I worked a part-time job during school and full time in the summer to pay for my personal expenses. I have informed them that they are welcome to purchase smartphones with their own money, which will require them to get jobs to earn their own money!

I consider it my parenting duty to teach them about working to earn things that they want. They both understand my stance, but they definitely don't like it.[4]

Even though I love this mother's approach, I'm not saying that we should all necessarily adopt the same tactic with our children. Every situation requires its own unique method and solution. The key is in understanding that giving in to every request that is not a true need doesn't bode well for your children, even when you can afford it. If you do, you're subconsciously teaching them a sense of entitlement. Eventually, when (not if) they run into a situation where someone doesn't

An entitled attitude is learned. It's something that we pick up from our surroundings, especially at a young age.

give them what they want, they will find it difficult to understand why. They'd feel they're being denied something that is rightfully theirs. They will feel someone owes them. And when somebody has the attitude that some other person owes them something, anger is not far away.

Something Owed

Anger happens to be one of the most destructive emotions that we experience. In many cases, anger comes from a heart that is devoid of humility. In his book *Enemies of the Heart*, Andy Stanley listed anger as one of the emotions that control us. He wrote, "The root of anger is the perception that something has been taken. Something is owed you."[5] The emphasis that "anger" places on the fact that you owe *me* and that restitution is required puts the focus on *me*. It's now about *me* and the injustice you have dealt *me* by denying *me* what is truly *mine*. This is having a high view of my own importance. This is entitlement. This is the opposite of humility.

To someone with a grateful attitude, there's no entitlement. They see what comes to them as gifts. These are gifts that they receive, not only with thankfulness, but also with a grateful heart. It's a heart that is magnified by a humble spirit. They don't feel that someone owes them something. Neither do they have an exaggerated view of their own importance. They don't expect others to do things for them just because they have a need and they feel others can meet that need.

When you're truly grateful, you're showing that there's no sense of entitlement. Your attitude is not one of expectation of what was done for you. You see what was done as a gift – a gift given, not earned. With a sense of entitlement however, you expect what's coming because you think you've earned it. It is rightfully yours and no one dare take it away or deny you the pleasure of it. Woe betides whoever tries!

Thankful vs. Grateful

As I've said before, I don't think being thankful equates to being grateful. However, I do believe that the path towards having an attitude of gratitude is laced with many instances of thankfulness. As we consistently show appreciation for what we have and the blessings that come our way, we begin to develop a grateful heart.

What are you thankful for today? I encourage you to take a moment to pause here and think about one thing for which you are thankful today. In fact, I implore you to start each day with an attitude of thankfulness. Take a few moments each morning to reflect and to focus on what you're thankful for. Contemplate these and count your blessings, instead of counting others' blessings.

> *Anger says "You owe me." It is the result of not getting something we want.*
>
> Andy Stanley

When you count other people's blessings instead of yours, it prevents you from seeing what's right in front of you.

Seeing the Invisible
A couple of months after I moved to the United States, I went to a Thai restaurant during a lunch break from work. This was my first time in this restaurant, and I enjoyed my experience there. When I was done, I paid my bill and walked out.

In the parking lot, just as I was about to get into my car, I felt a light tap on my right shoulder. I turned around to see the lady who had served me in the restaurant. She was breathing heavily; it seemed she must have been running after me. In her hand was the restaurant bill I had signed moments ago. She showed it to me and said, "You didn't add a tip!"

I was surprised as I restated the obvious. "Yes, I didn't."

Her next words shocked me. "You have to add a tip!"

My response? "No, I don't!"

But she insisted, "You must add a tip!"

I still couldn't believe what was going on, so I told her, "I thought tips were voluntary. You give tips if you want to, and you don't if you don't feel like it." Her reply further confused me.

"The workers in the restaurant get paid partly from the tips, so you must add a tip."

Now I was really getting annoyed. The whole experience just seemed unreal. However, because I did not want to argue with her any further, I added a tip to the receipt and gave it back to her. I left, still surprised that she forced me to add a tip against my will!

Before you start labeling me a terrible and stingy customer who denies service workers their tips wherever I go, please hear me out. Growing up in Nigeria, adding tips to food purchases were extremely rare. And this is because of the way we typically bought our meals.

First of all, most people cooked their meals in their own homes at that time (I believe that has changed now). We did not have a lot of "restaurants." Almost all of the places to buy cooked meals were makeshift sheds by the side of the road. We call these sheds *buka*. These places had no menus, and the food did not come with prescribed prices or in prepackaged quantities. When you bought food, you specified how much of each component of the meal you wanted. For example, you would say, "Give me 20 *naira* worth of rice; 10 *naira* of beans, and 10 *naira* of meats." When you collect your food, you pay exactly the amount owed. You never added tips!

The few places I learned about tips then were in big fancy restaurants that you typically find in five-star hotels. I had a couple of experiences with eating in these places because of the rare corporate lunches that we had at work when we took out colleagues visiting from Europe. In those instances, my boss would take everyone to lunch and he paid (with company funds, of course). Those were the rare cases where, when you would get a bill, you could include a tip if you felt like it. If you didn't feel like it, it was not a *Count your blessings, instead of counting others' blessings.* problem. This was the culture in which I grew up. That's what I knew about tips. That is, until the encounter I had at that Thai restaurant in St. Louis, Missouri.

Despite that experience, I went back to the restaurant for many years while living in St. Louis. I still go back there sometimes when I visit. In fact, the lady who ran after me eventually became a very good friend. I later found out she was a co-owner of the restaurant. Since that "tipping" experience, I try my best to tip as generously as possible at restaurants. I don't want someone chasing me down in the parking lot for a tip! Until that happened, I never gave any thought to the people who serve in those jobs. I definitely do now!

How about you? Do you give any thought to those who wait on you? It doesn't have to be only in restaurants, where a tip can be easily handed down. How about at the movie theatres, the post office, the grocery store, at the gym, and in many other places where we are served by others? Yes, these people are doing the jobs for which they are paid, but a little kindness shown towards them can go a long way to make someone's day. Many of us don't even see these people as they serve us. They're almost invisible to us. But imagine what a difference it could make if we took just a few moments of our time, as precious as it is to us, to acknowledge, appreciate, and recognize these people. I'm learning to make a conscious effort to do this more each day. I have to put in the effort to do this because it's not my natural tendency to do so.

These days, I look for opportunities to find people who are doing something that is often overlooked, walk up to them and thank them for doing their job. I have seen faces light up in those instances when I've remembered to do this. I'm sure you can do the same. All you need is a conscious awareness to put in the effort in seeing these people because they're around us every single day. As you do this, you're placing a premium on the importance of those who work to serve you. When you do this, you focus less on your view of your own importance. You begin to see how important others are, no matter how menial or trivial you may have considered what they do.

While my personal encounter at the Thai restaurant was due to my ignorance about the importance of tips to service workers, I have seen situations where ego and arrogance resulted in someone not leaving a tip at a restaurant. Take the example of this actual note that someone left on a restaurant bill instead of a tip. Here's what it said:

> "My tip is the freedom I provided you while serving
> my country. You're welcome for my service."

I definitely appreciate those who have served and who currently serve in various branches of the United States military. I'm thankful to them for risking their lives to provide the freedom and the protection we all enjoy. But I think this note takes entitlement to the highest levels of egotism. This note is a result of someone having a high view of their own importance to the detriment of others. It's a classic example of what not to do when we have an opportunity to give to others.

Giving to others and being socially responsible is a way that we acknowledge the importance of the people around us. We exhibit humility when we give out of our abundance or even in our lack. We may not have enough, but showing gratitude and giving out of our meagre resources shows our focus on the plight of those with whom we come into contact every day. It also shows our satisfaction with where we currently are, in our journey through life.

Contentment – An Inside Job

When my wife, our two boys, and I relocated to the United States in 1998, our third son was born immediately on arrival. It took less than two years before we were blessed with the opportunity to purchase our first home. Within a year of moving into the house, my daughter, our fourth child was born. To some around us, our home had suddenly become too small. But as a family, we were happy. We loved it. We were satisfied. On many occasions, the boys would leave their rooms to come and sleep with my wife and I in our bedroom. That meant all six of us slept in one room on most nights, thus leaving the other two bedrooms empty.

Even though we started praying for and began working towards having a bigger home with enough space for the children, my heart was full of unbridled gratefulness for what we had. In those days, my prayers always ended with "if this home is all we will ever have, I'm eternally grateful for its blessings." I was grateful because I knew we could easily be on the streets with no place to lay our heads. I also knew that most families do not get the chance to purchase a home in less than two years after moving from another country. We were beyond grateful for what we had. We lived in that house for seven years before our prayers were answered, and we moved into a bigger home, custom-built for us. Interestingly enough, we only lived in our new home for two years before we had to relocate to another state, but we had no problem leaving our dream home behind and moving on to the next exciting opportunity that was ahead for us.

Often, not being satisfied with what we have leads to a lack of gratitude. And usually, this lack of contentment is rooted in our comparison with what surrounds us. We look at our situation, and then compare it with those of others around us. If we fall short in that assessment, we run the risk of falling into the danger of being discontent.

In today's media-driven world, contentment has become increasingly hard to find and even harder to keep. There's always a newer, bigger, shinier, or prettier thing to desire, fawn over, and buy. In many cases, there's someone else who has what you want.

Over the last decade, the consumer electronics industry has cashed in big on these insatiable appetites. Many of us are willing to owe and make monthly payments for years just to get our hands on the latest gadgets. Ironically, this would last for just a few months before the next newer, bigger, shinier, or prettier version arrives, and the cycle is repeated. Discontent is everywhere you turn. Instead of people getting to live, they're living to get.

I once heard the late pastor and author Adrian Rogers define contentment as "an inner sufficiency that keeps us at peace in spite of outward circumstances." Contentment is an inner sufficiency. It's an inside job. Femi Awodele also echoed this when he told me that "contentment is the secret for peace in anyone's life."[6]

But let's not confuse being contented with complacency or being lazy. It has nothing to do with being self-satisfied, especially when there are opportunities for improvement staring you in the face. It also doesn't mean that you have enough possessions. Some can have more than enough things and still live in a continual state of dissatisfaction. And others can have very little and be satisfied. It takes neither riches nor poverty to learn contentment. How do you know that you may have problems with being contented? Let me illustrate with this exchange between two friends, Lucy and Joan.

Instead of people getting to live, they're living to get.

On hearing the doorbell ring, Lucy opened the door to welcome her friend Joan and her family. Lucy, her husband, and their three kids had just moved into their new home the previous week. Joan and her family were paying them a visit.

> **Lucy**: Welcome to our new home, guys! I hope you had no difficulty trying to find the place.
>
> **Joan**: Not at all! It was straightforward. Wow, what a lovely home! I love these window blinds!

Gratitude Is Key

Where did you get them?

Lucy: From the Big Furniture Store on Main Street. We had someone from the store come and install them for us.

Joan: I absolutely love them! I've been wanting the same type of blinds, but you know … they cost so much! We will get them once we have some extra cash.

As Lucy continued to show them around the house, there were many areas where Joan saw what she liked and wanted. A few of the times, she would turn to her husband and say, "Sam, we should get those when we have some extra money."

Finally, they got to the master bathroom. Joan screamed.

Joan: I absolutely loved this bathtub! It has all these water jets to massage your body as you take a bath! Sam, we should replace ours when we have some extra money.

Suddenly, Sam had had enough.

Sam: But honey, you chose the one we have now when our home was built just two years ago. I thought you said you really loved the one we have. And ours have water jets too!

Joan: Yes, I know, but this one is better! Can't you see that it has more jets than ours? Don't you want us to have better things?

Sam was furious with his wife, but said nothing further to prevent the situation from escalating into another conflict. And they've had many of those that came out of Joan's insatiable desire for whatever new thing she saw.

If like Joan, you're always seeing what you want from other people's stuff, you may be having contentment issues. I think it's okay to take ideas from others or allow their success to motivate you to learn, grow, and aspire for more in life. It becomes a problem when you're always wanting tangible things that others have. And the keyword here is *always*. This desire can easily lead to, or be the result of, envy, materialism, and greed. Instead of being grateful for what you have, you seem to always want something else that another person has.

For those who frequently use phrases such as "When I have more money …," "When I retire …," or "When the kids leave home …," they may eventually realize that many of these things they long for never materialize. What happens then, as time continues and none of what they ached for appears? They become filled with regrets about these unmet wants. In the process, their lives are cluttered with frequent bouts of dissatisfaction and unhappiness. That's because instead of looking at the blessings in their lives, they focus more on what they don't have and what they long for.

Please understand my heart here. I don't think there's anything wrong in wanting something better, especially in the area of personal growth and learning. In fact, I think every one of us should continue to work on becoming a better person in every area of our lives. But when it comes to possessions, we ought to be careful. I'm also not saying that it's bad to continue using old, dilapidated appliances and devices when you can get newer, more efficient ones. What I mean is that if you're not careful, you can easily fall into the trap of discontent when, on a regular basis, you strongly desire what you see others possess, instead of being grateful for what you already have.

One thing about always wanting more is its deceptive nature. It creeps into the heart unawares. In fact, it seems we humans are greedy and materialistic by nature. You don't believe me? Imagine this scenario that I first heard from Adrian Rogers about a toddler in a room full of toys. The toddler is playing with just one toy while all the other toys are scattered all over the room. Another child comes into the room, grabs one of the other toys to play with, and what do you see? Most of the time, the first child runs to the second and grabs that toy from him. Why? Because as Adrian Rogers said, "It's in our nature to be selfish and covetous. It doesn't matter what we have; we want that thing someone else has." So, this seems to be a natural human trait. You usually see these behaviors in children. As we grow older, some people learn the importance of being selfless and grateful. Unfortunately, there are some of us who do not.

The sad part about this is that those of us who remain like this tend not to see it in ourselves, but those around us do. If you're wondering whether or not you're guilty of this, just ask those who know you the best and you will get a good picture. Then, there are others who seem driven to achieve what they think is success in life, but on closer inspection, it's just a lot of attempts at being more important than others to the detriment of those around them. The consequences of behaviors like this can be deadly. Distrust, broken dreams, and ruined relationships are not too far from the peddlers of discontentment. That was what happened with Amy.

Amy was known to be enterprising and resourceful. She inherited a successful business from her mother, and she continued to build on that success every year. Despite how successful and influential she was, she had this insatiable desire to acquire wealth. She wanted to be seen with the movers and shakers in her city. She wanted to belong inside the "happening circle." As a result, she would dabble in anything and everything that seemed to be the current fad. If one of her friends achieved success in a particular line of business, that was the next thing Amy wanted to get into. Unfortunately, with each

A discontented man is never rich. A contented man is always rich.

Adrian Rogers

new thing that she attempted, success eluded her. Within a period of two years, she was involved in more than a dozen different types of businesses. Instead of focusing on her own lucrative business which was doing well, she wanted pieces of the pies from other businesses that her friends were successful in. After a while, these friends saw through her, especially when she started accusing them of not sharing the secrets to their successes. One by one, they deserted her. Before she knew what was happening, word got around that she was not the type of person to do business with. Soon, this began to affect her inherited once-lucrative, business. Before long, that business collapsed. She destroyed her own success and relationships because of greed and ingratitude.

Where discontentment and greed abound, lack of trust and

broken relationships will follow. Unfortunately, discontent is all around us today. It may even be celebrated in some cases. When a new version of iPhone is on the horizon, many with the current version begin to salivate and yearn for whatever new features the new one is supposed to have. I've seen a few of these people get into debt just to get their hands on the latest one. They want to belong in the group of those who can claim to have the newest version. Eventually, they get into trouble, either because of the mountain of debt they get into or the kinds of things they're willing to do for the latest device. They would do anything to be able to keep up with the Joneses. This level of greed is found in both the young and the old. Both the rich and the poor are afflicted with it. You find it among both the illiterate and the educated. Higher education doesn't cure it.

In their book, *The Abandoned Generation: Rethinking Higher Education*, William Willimon and Thomas Naylor wrote about a time when MBA students at Duke University's Fuqua School of Business were asked to respond to the question, "What do you want to be when you grow up?" In these authors' words, here's the summary of the responses from the students:[7]

> With few exceptions, they wanted three things – money, power, and things (very big things, including vacation homes, expensive foreign automobiles, yachts, and even airplanes). Primarily concerned with their careers and the growth of their financial portfolios, their personal plans contained little room for family, intellectual development, spiritual growth, or social responsibility.

> Their mandate to the faculty was, "Teach me how to be a money-making machine. Give me the facts, tools, and techniques required to ensure my instantaneous financial success." All else was irrelevant.

These future leaders already have their eyes set on having things – "very big things." Their goal in life, even while still in business school, was to acquire as much stuff as they could. But of course, they will discover that stuff doesn't really satisfy. In the end, your quality of life is not determined by the amount of junk that you have acquired. Your stuff doesn't define your worth. Your worth is determined in part by what you do to help others and to lift them up. When you reach the level of being contented no matter what you have or don't have, you have truly begun to live.

The good news is that we can learn to be content. It's as simple as being always thankful and shifting the focus of priorities from ourselves to other people. Here are a few simple things to practice daily.

1. *Be thankful.* I said this earlier in this chapter, and I'm repeating it here. Start each day with a reflective moment about what you're thankful for. Discontent results because of a constant focus on what you don't have instead of focusing on what you do have. When you count your blessings each day, your perception and attitude will begin to change.

2. *Shift your love of things to love of people.* Make a conscious effort to love people who have more than you and who have what you don't. Remind yourself that their blessing is not your loss. It's not a zero-sum game. In addition, find ways to add value to people with whom you come into contact every day.

3. *Share what you have.* Learn to give to others. Many of us hold tightly to what we have because we think we don't have enough. No matter how little you have, there's always someone who has less than you. Giving doesn't have to be about tangible things. You can give of your time or attention to someone who needs them.

I recently learned about the Japanese term, "*on*". I was told that it means having a sense of gratitude that is accompanied by a desire to repay others for what you have been given. You're not repaying others because of what they have done for you. You're repaying them because of the blessings you have received. So, this goes beyond just being grateful, or expressing gratitude. It's about truly experiencing a sincere desire to give something back in order to make the world a better place just because you have the means to do so. Personally, I think this may have been the idea behind "The Giving Pledge".

Started in August 2010 by Bill Gates, Melinda Gates, and Warren Buffett, "the Giving Pledge came to life following a series of conversations with philanthropists around the world about how they could collectively set a new standard of generosity among the ultra-wealthy."[8] The concept behind it is relatively simple. It's "an open invitation for billionaires, or those who would be if not for their giving, to publicly commit to giving the majority of their wealth to philanthropy." These billionaires were inspired to do this by the kind of example they see in ordinary people all over the world, who give generously to make the world a better place, often at great personal sacrifices.

People who want what others have, don't seem to be thankful for the gifts they have been given.

Dr. Melba Hooker

Why would anyone do this, you may ask? Think of it as a sense of obligation that arises from having a deep gratitude and appreciation from the blessings you have received. It's not an externally imposed obligation. No one forces you to do it. Instead, it follows a sense of responsibility that arises naturally within us, as we recognize how we have been blessed and cared for by others throughout our entire lives.

Without contentment, you most definitely would not have that deep sense of appreciation for what you've been given. As a result, there are those who, in addition to not being appreciative, do not see the value in what has been done for them. This in turn, could lead to repaying the good with bad.

Bad for Good

Have you ever done something good for someone and they neither acknowledged what you had done nor shown any gratitude? (And all the parents of ungrateful children said, *Amen!*) Or maybe, if they responded at all, it was with disdain and rudeness in their reaction to what you had done? How about a situation where a good deed that you did for someone was repaid with bad? Just imagine how that makes you feel!

You've gone out of your way to do something for someone out of the goodness of your heart. You didn't have to do it. But you did it anyway because you saw that they had a need and you wanted to help. And what did you get in return? Scorn, disdain, and contempt for your efforts. Such a "reward" for a good deed can bring out the worst reaction from even the most genial of folks. Even now, I can only imagine the type of feelings just reading the last few sentences are evoking in some of you. You want to yell! Or maybe slap some sense into someone! I want to share a few real examples of this with you so you can see the effects of not being grateful on those we associate with.

While serving at a homeless shelter one day, Melba was serving a chicken dinner to a displaced gentleman when she heard the man complain about the chicken. She felt like screaming, but held herself together. The dinner was free, she thought. "If you didn't care for any of the menu items, take what you like and be silent!"[9] That's what she wanted to say, but didn't. She later confided in me that she was just as embarrassed by her unspoken response as she was by the man's ungrateful rant. She felt that she could have responded differently and with humility.

Have you experienced something similar to this? What's your story? What happened? How did you respond? What feelings were you left with?

Nair was left with feelings of distrust after she opened up her home to someone in need and got a bad rap in the process. In her own words:

> I met this lady who had lost a child and was dealing with severe depression. I opened my home to her and spent a lot of time with her, even more than what I was normally comfortable with. I thought that she needed help and that I should try my best to be there for her.
>
> Later, I learned from a longtime friend that she

was saying all kinds of negative things about me. She said that I was trying to take advantage of her situation so she could take care of my kids. She even criticized the way I was raising my children. To make the situation worse, she said all these things to my friend, but nothing to me!

I was really sad when this happened. When I do something for someone, I don't expect them to repay the favor, but it was really hurtful for her to say those false and negative things about someone that was there for her when she needed it. I thought she was the one taking advantage of me. I then knew that she was a dishonest person; someone I can't trust.[10]

If you were Nair, would you trust this person?

Mary told me the story of a pastor who, along with his wife used their own money to purchase groceries for a family in need. Although the family attended their church, this gesture was a personal sacrifice for them because it wasn't as if they had a lot themselves. After they had delivered the groceries and left, a member of the family called the pastor on the phone. He was expecting them to simply say "thank you." Instead, the response from the family was "Pastor, you forgot the butter."[11] What gall?! What audacity?! It wasn't as if the family gave the pastor and his wife a grocery list! Even if they had given them a list and an item was missing, I thought the more appropriate response should have been to simply say thanks. But that's not what happened.

How would you have responded to that ingratitude if you were that pastor and his wife? It's amazing for me to discover that situations similar to this are very common. I'm sure you can think of at least one that's happened to you. Here are some of the actual examples that people wrote to me about:

You loaned someone money, but they never repaid it. You lend your car to someone in need, and it was returned with a cracked windshield or a broken taillight with no explanation as to what happened. How about a not-too-distant relative who's always asking you for money but never shows any appreciation because they feel you had the resources to always give to them? You gave a ride to someone who was stranded on a lonely road at night, and they accuse you of stealing from them the next day. Or worse, they rob you of your car or other valuables! You provide free lodging to a family in need for a few months, and they trash and destroy your property before leaving. You try to lend a helping hand, and you were shamed in response. As a teacher, you spend your own money to buy supplies for your students and get fired from your teaching job as a reward. You stood as the guarantor for a loan and the person defaulted; now you're liable. You reach out to befriend someone who was lonely, and they gossip and lie about you.

The list is endless. You can add yours. I'm almost certain that you can remember something good you have done for others that was repaid with bad.

All of these experiences leave you with one type of disappointment or the other. You felt betrayed and used for the unpaid loan. You were angry because of the cost to replace your car windshield or fix the broken tail light. You felt used by the thanklessness of the relative who's like a leech that's sucking the life out of you. You felt betrayed and deeply hurt after being played like a fiddle for offering a helping hand. Your mouth is left with the sour taste of trying to repay another person's loan . . . and on and on it goes.

These are the results of the behaviors from those who think highly of themselves. Such are the actions of those who have a high view of their own importance. It's not enough for them to *not* show gratitude for the good thing done for them, they rub your goodness in your face by the way they respond. They repay your kindness with either disdain or evil. And it's because they consider themselves too important. They're so important that you did not do enough for them. Your kindness did not meet the high level of excellence that their awesomeness deserves! You did not do justice to their sense of self-importance!

As appalling and distasteful as many of these behaviors may seem, some of us are the actual perpetrators. Are you one of those? Am I? Do your reactions to acts of kindness done for you leave bad tastes in people's mouths? Even if these are not normal patterns of behavior for you, do you occasionally fall into this trap and behave this way? This is something you and I need to think about. When we behave this way, it's our ego and selfishness that is at work. Unfortunately, some of us don't even realize the impact of these behaviors on others. We may not have enough self-awareness to see how our behaviors affect those around us.

A Likeable Attraction

One key point many people devoid of an attitude of gratitude fail to see, is how it makes them look. Ingratitude could make whiners out of its peddlers. And whining is not a very attractive trait.

Eric and John were childhood buddies. They grew up in the same neighborhood, attended the same elementary and middle schools, and shared many good memories growing up. Their interests were similar, and they both agreed to become engineers when they grow up. They even decided

A grateful mind is a great mind which eventually attracts to itself great things.

Plato (423 – 348 BC)

on which college they would attend. But as they were about to start high school, John's family moved away. As a result, they ended up attending different high schools in separate cities. Still, they kept in touch.

True to their words, both of them applied to the college they had agreed on attending. Both were offered admission to that college to study the same major. Each one was brilliant and they excelled in their studies and extracurricular activities.

As the end of their second year in college drew near, Eric noticed a strange pattern starting to emerge with John. Eric realized that each time there was a test, mid-term or final exam, John was always trying to compare exact grades even when both get the same letter grade, which for them was usually an A.

> **John**: Eric, I see that you got 99% on the mid-term. I got 97%.
>
> **Eric**: Yes, that's good! We both got an A. Isn't that cool?

Gratitude Is Key

John: Yes, it is. But your A is higher.

Eric: What's the difference? We've both been getting A's since elementary school and our GPAs are the same.

John: Yes, I know. But you consistently do better than me. I don't know why I'm not as smart as you. You always do better!

Eric: Really? What about the class last semester when you had 98% and I got 97%?

John: Well, that's the only time. Even then, the difference was slimmer than when you got higher grades.

Eric: It's the same grade. We both got A's!

John: Yes, but ...

Eventually, Eric concluded that there was no pleasing John. Soon, he started avoiding him. After a while, he became anxious about hanging out with his friend or even running into him on campus. Sometimes, when he saw him coming from afar, he would turn around or change direction so they don't meet. Before long, the divide became wider and wider. By the time they graduated, they were barely on speaking terms.

When someone is not satisfied with what they have, they tend to whine and complain. As they do this, people around them are repelled. Who wants to hang around someone who's always complaining and grumbling about how things are better for you compared to them?

On the contrary, when someone is full of gratitude, it becomes a magnet that attracts good things. Just think about it. Would you want to hang out with anyone who seems to always complain and whine? Or are they easier to be around when they are relaxed and expressing gratitude? The answer is obvious, isn't it?

When you show gratitude, either to others or just for what you have, it endears you to those around you. You are portrayed in positive light because being grateful brings positive energy. And positive energy is like a magnet. It attracts.

The attraction that gratitude brings is not only to people, but to a whole lot more. With gratitude and the resultant positive energy, you're motivated to action. Consistent action and learning will bring positive results, which will further improve your positive outlook on life. Gratitude improves morale and therefore will lead you to being more productive in whatever you do.

Moreover, when we're grateful, we tend to be generous. Unbridled generosity usually flows out of a grateful heart. And what is more attractive to people than generosity? Nothing! You're never more attractive to people than when you are generous to them; when you give of your time, money and other resources to them.

Some may think that being grateful is just a fuzzy thing that cannot be truly quantified. Contrary to this, there are multiple research reports that show that the benefits of cultivating an attitude of gratitude are very real. In her blog, [13]*The Science of Gratitude: More Benefits Than Expected*, Amit Amin has cataloged[12] a few of those studies that show the real tangible benefits of being grateful.

As we learn to be grateful, we're also learning to be humble because the focus is not on us and our wants. Our focus shifts to others and their needs. When that happens, we cease to see ourselves as lofty and high, compared to others. We begin to change our conceited view of our own importance. With that shift in focus, we have a clearer and better view of the future.

The Grateful Optimist
One of the things I've come to realize is how much gratitude affects the way we see and engage in the future. That's because when you're grateful, a lot of things fall into their proper perspectives. You see things with more clarity. And you're likely to be more optimistic about what the future holds.

Optimism is an important and powerful trait that can go a long way in determining the difference between success and failure in life. As I have studied optimism over the years and taught it in seminars as a strong component of emotional intelligence, I've become convinced of its power to shape whether or not you and I experience victory in our daily lives.

What exactly is optimism? I've heard people say that they're just not optimistic. They say it that way as if optimism is a personality trait. But it's not. It's a skill that you can learn. It's a skill that I believe is strongly rooted in our ability to show gratitude. Optimism is an indicator of a positive outlook. It's simply a choice to look at the brighter side of life. It is having a positive attitude especially when facing adversity. It is the dogged determination to remain hopeful and resilient when everything around you may be crumbling.

It's a fact of life that both good and bad things happen to everyone. No one has it rosy all the time. You may be thinking that you know people who seem to have it all together and whose life may seem to be perfect in every way. I can assure you that this is very far from reality. Everyone knows where their shoe pinches. And unless you're wearing their shoes, you don't feel the pinch. You feel the pinch in your shoes. They feel theirs. No one can really tell how good or bad things are for others. Each person knows their own.

Since good and bad happens to everyone, how we see them and then respond tend to determine how successful we become. The one we choose to focus on looms large. The problem is that most of us have the tendency to gravitate towards, and focus on, the negatives in our lives. We dwell on the bad – our losses, what's going wrong, what's not working, what we don't have. When this happens consistently, it can lead us down the road to becoming pessimistic. We then see our lives as an unending series of misfortunes and failures from which there's no way out. But we can also choose to focus on the positives – our gains, what's going right, what's working, what we do have. Sometimes, the same situation that brings pain could also bring joy, but you have to see the joy beneath the pain. It was Jean-Baptiste Alphonse Karr who said, "Some people are always grumbling because roses have thorns; I am thankful that thorns have roses." It's simply what you choose to focus on.

NOTHING HIGHER

Focusing on the good gives you the power, strength, and motivation needed to turn things around. Instead of being drained by wallowing in your misery, you receive boosts of energy to get things done and achieve success. It's a choice you and I have to make. It's an individual choice. It's the choice Gary made after an unfortunate accident more than twenty years ago.

It happened in February 2000. Gary was in the car with his son on Interstate 80 when their car rolled over multiple times. The accident left him paralyzed from the chest down. Almost eighteen years later as he sat with me, recollecting the events from a few weeks after the accident, I heard the heart of a man who made the choice not to dwell on the bad, but to focus on the good. Here's what he told me:

> After the surgeries, I remember just reflecting and singing out loud how grateful I was for all the incredible times I'd had while I was walking and until I'm walking again one day. At that time, it would seem in the natural like the lowest point ever to me.
>
> My son was pushing me around in the courtyard – it was probably about twelve to fifteen days after that accident. And I was just saying to him, "Remember the time we got to do this, and we climbed that. Wasn't that awesome?! Remember all the times we played basketball in the driveway together," which was half an hour to an hour every day. And talking to my daughter and asking her, "Remember the times we got to play? We had so many good times." And talking to my wife saying, "You remember when we got to do this together?"
>
> I found that those moments actually gave me strength. Instead of thinking, "Oh! Poor, pitiful me! I'm paralyzed," but more like, "Wow! What a full life I've had!" Think about the things I've been able to do that few people ever get to do. I've been so incredibly blessed. I know it gave me

60

strength.[13]

With what happened to Gary, it would be easy for him to be weighed down by the hand fate had dealt him. I don't think anyone would blame him for that. But he chose to look at the situation differently. Recollections about what he was able to do before the accident would have brought untold sorrow to others. But to him, it was a source of joy and strength. Instead of lamenting the things he couldn't do anymore, he remembered with fondness that he was able to do those things. *"What a full life I've had! Think about the things I've been able to do that few people ever get to do. I've been so incredibly blessed."* This is thankfulness! This is what a grateful heart looks like.

With a heart of gratitude, Gary Hoyt continued to serve in his role as the Lead Pastor of Bellevue Christian Center for another twenty years after the accident until his retirement. His heart, passion, and outlook in life is a testimony to what God can do with a grateful heart. It's an incredible privilege for me to call this man my friend and mentor. As a leader full of integrity and gratitude, his life continues to touch and transform others wherever he goes.

What You Get
Here's a summary of the benefits that come to you when your humility shines forth in gratitude.

1. You actually begin to live life to the fullest. Being grateful brings peace and joy to your daily living. Instead of worrying about what you don't have and being weighed down by the resulting negative emotions, you're focusing on the positives in your life. These will bring bursts of positive emotions that will help you achieve more in life.

2. It attracts others to you. People want to be around you, work with you, help you and do life with you. And you can't do life alone. You need others to help you get to greater heights.

3. With gratitude, you see things clearly and with the proper perspectives. Even when challenges come,

you're able to remain optimistic and face those
obstacles with hope and resilience.

What You Can Do
When it comes to ingratitude, examples abound all around us.
There's one aspect in particular that I've seen many times. If you
travel a lot for business, you may complain about crowded
airports, rental cars with little space for your luggage, stuffy and
dingy hotel rooms, complimentary hotel breakfasts not having
what you'd like to eat, or the hotel not providing complimentary
Wi-Fi. On the other hand, if your job doesn't involve any travel,
you may complain about not going anywhere interesting, of being
bored, of not having anything good to watch on TV. It doesn't
matter where we are or what we do, some of us always seem to
find something to complain and grumble about.

As I said before, all we need to start cultivating an attitude of
gratitude is a shift in our focus. It is a function of attention. It's
not dependent on your situation. It's about what you choose to
focus on. Start by focusing less on what you don't have and begin
paying attention to what you do have. Think about what's going
right in your life instead of paying attention to what is going
wrong. Focus on your gains instead of focusing on your losses.
Just adjust your focus a little. You can do this through an
intentional and deliberate act of daily self-reflection. The
following are a few simple steps you can take:

1. Start each day with a moment of contemplation,
    introspection, and self-reflection. Begin by focusing
    on what you are thankful for. We tend to take a lot of
    things for granted, especially those things which
    come to us regularly and without effort. For example,
    you can give thanks for the fact that you're alive and
    able to breathe freely and easily without help. There
    are people who cannot breathe without assistance.

2. Think about people in your sphere of influence to
    whom you can show love and kindness. Reflect on
    what you can do for them as an expression of that

love, and then act on it! When we express gratitude to others through words and deeds, our experience of gratefulness is enriched.

3. Think about the good fortunes that others have received and be thankful for them. Don't complain about what they have and you don't. If you're prone to constantly complaining, and you're looking for how to stop, I recommend an interesting website by Will Bowen called, *AComplaintFreeWorld.org*.

4. Think about people you can do something for, and add value to. Use your knowledge of them to go out of your way to do something extraordinary for them. Seek to always give rather than receive. Receiving things from others is good but we should not be actively seeking to get from others. Instead, look for opportunities to give and be a blessing to others.

Finally, even in instances when you're thankful, how do you communicate that? In most cases, gratitude can be expressed in both words and actions. If we're not careful however, some of our pronouncements and behaviors can seriously take away from our quest to be humble. Sometimes, arrogance can masquerade under the guise of gratitude. You may use words that articulate how grateful you are, but your real intentions could be to flaunt your accomplishments. Walter Hooker pondered this with me when he asked, "Am I thankful that I did this, or I'm thankful for what God has done for me or how He has used me? Are you grateful for other people? Are you thankful for the good job other people are doing versus what you're doing?"[14]

So, even though expressing gratitude usually shows humility, some of our other expressions can take away from this and make us less humble.

CHAPTER 4
CIVIL EXPRESSIONS

Immodest words admit of no defense,
For want of modesty is want of sense.
                                    - Alexander Pope

S everal years ago, I was at a wedding reception near Oakland, California. This reception was for a Nigerian couple and, as many Nigerians know, such occasions are tailor-made for introductions and speeches. A typical Nigerian wedding reception is somewhat different, even when it's taking place in North America. There's usually a chairperson for the event, and this person gets invited to sit at the head table along with the new couple and a few other people.

As the master of ceremony introduced the chairman at this particular wedding reception, he had the audacity to refer to him as *"Doctor Mike Michaels"* (that's not his real name). As soon as he arrived at the table, he grabbed the microphone from the master of ceremony and emphatically declared that his name was *Chief, Doctor, Professor, Mike Michaels*.

This may seem ridiculous to my Western friends, but this is fairly common in many parts of Africa. My African friends won't find it funny as I dare say that in Africa, we love our titles! We love the applause. We want the recognition.

I can recollect a time in Nigeria, when the battle raged for engineers to be recognized with the prefix "Engineer (or Engr.)" before their names. Doctors do it after all! They're referred to as "Doctor So and So." Why can't engineers enjoy a similar recognition? Lawyers have theirs too: "Barrister ..." And before long, we also had "Accountant ...," "Magistrate ...," and a whole list of prefixes that goes before people's names. The funny thing is that you only see this when people have had a good college education, and they want to flaunt it. Hey, it's probably a good idea to have everyone's profession added as a prefix to their names. That way, we'd get to know the person and their profession in one sentence instead of two! But I very much doubt that people being introduced as "Carpenter Bob Roberts" or "Plumber Bill Williams" will ever catch on!

Just as introductions by third parties make us known to others, our own speech and other expressions can quickly provide ways for people to know us. I believe that the manner in which you and I express ourselves to others can go a long way to expose whether or not we have a high view of our own importance. To be clear, when I say the manner in which we express ourselves, I'm not just referring to speech. Neither am I alluding to differences in personality. That's because when it comes to expressing ourselves, there are times when we confuse people's personality with humility. Someone who is quiet and reserved in nature can sometimes be mistaken for being humble. And this could be very far from the truth! At the other end of the spectrum, those whose personalities make them gregarious and more expressive may be seen as prideful. This may also be incorrect. So, while our communications can reflect either pride or humility, care must be taken not to confuse this with personality type differences.

Bad Taste
Here's what I know. Those prefixes before your first name, (and sometimes, the long string of letters and acronyms that show your educational achievements after your last name), do not really define who you are. They may show your accomplishments, but it's not the real you. Your parents (or whoever gave you your name) did not call you that. They may have appended a few letters (Jr.) or some Roman numerals (II, III or IV) to show that you're

not the first to bear your name in the family, but that's it. Many of us see our identities in what we do or what we have accomplished, but who you are goes deeper than that.

Don't get me wrong! I'm not saying it's bad to acknowledge what you have accomplished. In fact, denying our accomplishments tend to have a similar negative effect – we will touch on that later. But, in my opinion, when those self-aggrandizing words come out of your mouth, your audience is actually hearing what you don't want them to hear. While the words may be sweet in your mouth, they are distasteful and repugnant to the ears of many listening to you. All that it does, is leave a bad taste in their mouth. Or more appropriately, a terrible sound in their ears! The result is the exact opposite of what you're looking for. That's because when you seek the applause, you actually cease the applause. You may receive the physical act of people slapping their hands together for you, but you're not getting the true ovation that comes from hearts filled with genuine appreciation for you.

It's true that we all indulge in occasional boastings now and then. It develops into a problem however, when this becomes a pattern which people can easily identify with you. Psychologists believe that this could be the result of low self-esteem. When self-esteem is low, it can lead to the need to visibly amplify your own image, and it ends up being done in a pompous and arrogant manner.

Boasting about yourself does a lot more damage than you can imagine. While those who do this tend to do so to puff up their image, what they end up doing is destroying the very image they're trying to improve. Unfortunately, they may not even know what the damaging effects are. The

When you seek the applause, you cease the applause.

unspoken expectation of those around us is to be modest. When we boast, we violate this expectation.

Many who brag do so to change or manage other's impressions about them. In a 2012 blog published in *Psychology Today*, Dr. Susan Krauss Whitbourne, a professor of psychology at the

University of Massachusetts, wrote about how we can use bragging with caution. This author of "The Search for Fulfillment" defined Impression Management[1] as being "all about leading others to view you favorably. If they think you're trying too hard, they'll be turned off and you'll achieve exactly the opposite of your desired impact on others. This is especially true if the qualities you're showing off aren't the ones that interest the other person."

While it may be counter-intuitive, I think the best way to brag about yourself is not to brag at all. If you're as good as you think you are, others will do the bragging for you. The wise King Solomon once said, "Let another praise you, and not your own mouth; a stranger, and not your own lips." When other people see something worth emulating in you or about you, and they laud you, whether in public or in private, it carries a lot more weight than whatever you are inclined to say about yourself. These days however, social media has turned this around. We now have several outlets for tooting our own horn whenever we feel like it.

Social or Anti-Social
The rise in the popularity of social media over the last decade has made the practice of trumpeting our own accomplishments commonplace. Someone once told me about a post from one of her Facebook friends. She recalled the post as saying something along the lines of:

> I have a good life, good relationships, good job.
> Everything about me is fantastic. Thank you,
> Lord![2]

The comments written in response by her "friends" on Facebook were brutal! Some said she was proud. Others said if she truly possessed all she had listed, she would not have posted the comments. Many more accused her of lying. In fact, many of the comments were so negative that she had to eventually delete the post.

Most of us have our reasons for posting whatever it is that we post on social media. At the same time, each of us sees other people's posts announcing their accomplishments through different lenses. What some see as sharing, others may see as showy or bragging. I receive a wide range of responses when I polled opinions on why people post what they have accomplished online.

Although he doesn't post such things online, Yemmy believes some do this as a sense of fulfillment or to flow with what their friends, acquaintances or coworkers are doing online. He also thinks there are people who do it just to show off. On the other side of the coin, he thinks others do not post simply because they "don't fancy the need to make noise over their accomplishments."[3]

On the other hand, Melba reasons that some people's posts are simply "to demonstrate their pursuit of excellence in their field," even though she doesn't post such. She also thinks that "a false sense of humility may hinder some from sharing those accomplishments." Ouch! As scathing as that sounds, I would agree. She believes that "the testimony of my clients should speak for my work and character."[4]

Bob thinks the current technology-enabled, mobile culture has eroded the closeness of the nuclear family. As a result, "we turn to our extended virtual family for the validation we used to receive around the dinner table."[5] Nair agrees, because she believes many who post

Let another praise you, and not your own mouth; a stranger, and not your own lips.

King Solomon

such do so because "they need recognition of their success or their achievements from others." Her thought was that these people are insecure, and they "need to show others what they have accomplished in order to feel good about themselves."[6]

This is something that I think should be of major concern to everyone, especially parents of impressionable teenagers. Seeking validation for one's self-worth from strangers – and many Facebook friends are just that – can cause serious damage to the emotional health of such individuals. I do realize that for most of us, our accomplishments will never be on the evening news broadcast, so many people may not know about them, especially our multitude of "friends" on Facebook or "followers" on any other social media platform. As a result, some of us feel the need to share the good news so others can rejoice with us. I get this. And I think we should rejoice with those who rejoice. However, when we share our own accomplishments, I think there's a very fine line between sharing something that can motivate others and the appearance of being boastful. I have found out that when those closest to you know about something you've achieved and they post such online, congratulating you, it seems to carry more weight in the eyes of others than when you post those accomplishments yourself. For example, I personally find it odd when I see someone post "Happy birthday to me!" on their own Facebook page. I'm not saying it's wrong; I just find it unusual. I understand it's a way to let people know it's their birthday, but it still doesn't sound normal because in typical conversations, you don't usually hear people saying "Happy birthday to me," to others that they come across on their special day.

> *We turn to our extended virtual family for the validation we used to receive around the dinner table.*
>
> Bob McCoy

I think blowing our own trumpet says something about how either significant or insignificant we think we are. Personal experience has shown me that many who tend to announce their accomplishments or acquisitions on the mountain tops (of social media) do so because they want to shore up their significance in the minds of others. This doesn't mean that they're not important or significant; the problem may be their own perception of their significance. I believe that if these people have the right view of themselves, they're not likely to want to seek validation from others. This reminds me of the words in the chorus of the song, *Who I Am* by Blanca Elaine Callahan. In the last line of that chorus, she sang about knowing who she is when she knows whose she is.

I wholeheartedly agree with Blanca. When we truly know whose we are, then we will have the right perspective of who we are. Otherwise, even the significance that we may think we're getting from others' responses to our posts is probably only skin deep. Almost everyone who responded to my questions on this issue agreed that many of the comments from Facebook "friends" on these types of posts are insincere at best. So why go through the trouble when the outcomes of such endeavors are really the opposite of what is desired? Maybe those who seek such validation just don't care.

This can be an emotional or sensitive subject for many of us because we post things about ourselves on social media all the time. It can even be controversial because many of us may feel strongly about this, one way or another. I know that it's a sore point for many because of the wide range of responses that I received from those who answered my questions on this topic.

Here's what I ask of you. Think and ask yourself why you want to post what you're about to post online. Is it to boast, to provide information, or to express gratitude? You are the only person who can truly answer that for yourself. All I ask is that you be honest with yourself. I believe we can all do that if we choose to. A very good friend wrote me to say, "My husband, who I consider to be a confident and intelligent person, spends what I consider to be a ridiculous amount of time crafting *Think, and ask yourself why you want to post what you're about to post online.* certain Facebook post announcements to ensure he gives the right 'vibe' that is not too self-focused but still communicates what he wants people to know." I say kudos to the nameless husband of this woman! He uses the platform to communicate what he wants, but has enough self-awareness to avoid situations where his posts could appear as self-glorification.

Here's a basic test that I apply. I ask myself before I post anything, "Does posting this focuses attention on me and what I've done? If it focuses on me, am I giving information that people would need and appreciate? Or does it give credit to (or recognize) someone other than me?" My responses to these questions help me decide whether or not I should post whatever it is, or if I need to re-write the posting. I think your honest responses to these questions will do the same for you.

You probably know that not all boastings happen online through social media. There are different avenues through which the incurable braggart can peddle his or her wares. In professional settings, this search for significance can rear its ugly head in different ways. It could make someone speak out of turn in a meeting just because of this tendency to draw attention to themselves. The result could make them look and sound more foolish than if they had simply kept quiet.

It's All About Me

Mike was a brilliant salesperson. Charismatic and personable, his sales numbers were off the charts five years in a row. He won every award you could think of, both within his organization and nationally. In fact, his performance was also responsible for his team winning multiple awards. He was the one that carried the team for all those years. He was really good at what he did. His customers loved him, and they kept coming back to him.

Despite his charisma and the loyal effect this had on his customers, there was a side of him that they never saw. It was an ugly side that his coworkers knew very well, and which they saw on a daily basis – his constant boasting and bragging about his accomplishments. As a result, most of his colleagues either avoided him or treated him with disdain.

For people like Mike who indulge in self-adulation, their primary goal is for others to have a high opinion about them. What they fail to realize however, is how annoying and irritating that behavior comes across to others. According to the results of a research published in the June 2015 edition of *Psychological Science,*[7] "People overestimate the extent to which recipients of their self-promotion will feel proud of and happy for them, and underestimate the extent to which recipients will feel annoyed." Because of this miscalculation, the result they get is the opposite of what they had hoped for.

As I noted earlier, the pervasiveness of social media can make the consequences of this behavior immediate and more dramatic. For example, sharing information about your recent promotion, or posting a photo of your brand-new car or house on Facebook, may seem like innocent ways to share the good news. But studies and experience show that this often backfires. That's what Patrick experienced.

After landing a good job, Patrick and his wife, Kristen, were able to buy a house in California, where they live with their three children. Soon, he bought a big car – an SUV – for himself, and not too long thereafter, he bought another for his wife. With each of these purchases, an announcement followed on Facebook with photos showing every nook and cranny of their home and the vehicles. Each post received many "likes" and congratulatory comments. On social media, the comments were mostly positive. What Patrick did not realize is the effect that his constant posting about his latest acquisitions were having on those closest to him.

During their monthly extended family get-together for dinner, Patrick would tell anyone who cared to listen about how expensive his home and SUVs were. His brothers, sisters, and cousins, along with their families, would sit silently through each episode. Thinking that they were truly listening to him, Patrick did not notice the yawns that expressed their boredom, or how they avoided eye contact with him. He was insensitive to (or simply refused to recognize) the abundance of negative body language that tried to drown his voice each time. Eventually, it was his wife, who had had enough of his constant boasting when she spoke up suddenly one evening. "Yes, we get it! We have a lot of good things!" The tone with which Kristen spoke caught him by surprise, snapping him back to reality.

Here's what I think. When you brag about what you possess or have achieved, you're putting yourself on a pedestal. You're communicating your high view of your own importance. You're effectively saying, "I'm better than you." You elevate yourself above others. This creates a gap in your relationship with others. The more you engage in this behavior, the greater the distance between you and those with whom you're supposed to be doing life. Other studies[8] have shown that most people have a limited ability to recognize how their efforts at boasting and self-promotion adversely affect their acceptance and likeability by others, which is their original goal.

NOTHING HIGHER

If you're given to this type of behavior, the way you view and speak about your success could also eventually lead to a slippery slope towards unethical behaviors. Because of your success, you may think that you can get away with anything. But this may come back to haunt you. This reminds me of the story of a pharmaceutical salesman who was fired for some of the boastful contents he had written in a book while working for a previous employer.

When you brag, … you create a gap in your relationships with others.

In March 2005, Eli Lilly fired an employee who wrote a book in which he had boasted about how little he worked and how much money he earned while he was a sales representative at a previous company.[9] In his book, he spoke about how he exaggerated the frequency of his visits to doctors' offices and how he would order extra food (on the company's dime) while visiting physicians in order to have leftovers to take home for dinner.

The report claimed that this oblivious employee was surprised by Eli Lilly's decision to fire him because of actions he took while with another employer. He reportedly said, "I can see where people may say it was unethical but I was still making my numbers." From that statement, we can conclude that, to him, making his numbers was more important than the manner in which he made those numbers. In his mind, the end justified the means. This is a common attitude that comes with having a high view of one's own importance. To this salesman, his importance was determined by "making his numbers." As far as he was concerned, that was all that mattered. Nothing else did. "Making his numbers" had elevated him to the levels that others can only aspire to. But his employers disagreed. And they got rid of him even though what he had described actually happened with a previous employer. To Eli Lilly, this spoke volumes about his character.

Since boasting about yourself looks bad, you may think that going to the other extreme end of the spectrum and shying away from speaking out is the preferred way to go. You would be wrong if that's what you think.

74

Civil Expressions

What Are You Afraid Of?

I once heard someone define FEAR as *False Evidence Appearing Real*. For many of us, however, the experience of fear is very real. Almost every one of us is afraid of something. Fear has been with us since the beginning of time. Unless you're not human, you experience fear of one kind or another. This fear can appear and show up in different forms; some of them not easily identifiable. Can you identify your fears? Do you know what you're afraid of?

If you do an internet search for what most of us are afraid of, you get a dizzying array of results with the following five appearing near the top of most lists of phobias.

- Public Speaking (glossophobia)
- Flying (aerophobia)
- Death (thanatophobia)
- Heights (acrophobia)
- Spiders (arachnophobia)

To some of us, a few of these phobias or many on the *Ultimate List of Phobias and Fears*[10] may seem irrational – such as the fear of *people* or fear of *feet*. But when you think about it, what you are afraid of may seem irrational to others also. One person's phobia is another's absurdity!

Interestingly enough, my own surveys about fears yielded none on the list of the five common phobias I've just listed. The fears expressed by my respondents were much more profound than I had expected. They carried deeper meanings. I'm indebted to these people who were able to share their deepest and scariest doubts and worries. As I share some of those fears here, I won't be using their names unless they expressly gave me permission. My goal in sharing these is the hope that you can feel encouraged by some of them, because many of us tend to feel that we are alone in our fears and insecurities.

One person wrote to tell me about her fear of failure and disappointment. In her mind, these two are connected. Not liking to be disappointed, she's afraid to fail and thereby disappoint others, perhaps even others of which she may be unaware. To address this fear, she tries to be diligent to perform every task excellently. Similarly, my good friend, César, who lives in Clayton, North Carolina is afraid of not being there for his family. He said, "Because I grew up in a culture that says that I need to be my family's provider, I'm always second-guessing my decisions to ensure that they're the best decisions for my family."[11]

Then, there are other times when we fear something that has already happened to us; the feelings that came out of it are not necessarily what we would want to experience again. That was the case with Julia (not her real name) who told me that her two greatest fears are failure and being abandoned by the people she trusts most. She said, "those are my two biggest fears because I have experienced both, and both have been the worst experiences of my life. I do not wish to experience either one again." This is similar to the fear of an imminent or impending loss. Jacquie spoke to me about the fear of losing her mom. Even though her mother was alive at the time she told me this, she was scared of losing her because of all the challenges her mom had recently gone through. She said her mom "has been such a support, encourager, and listener" in her life. She continued, "My mother now has dementia, so we do not talk in the same way, and I already feel the loss."[12] Jacquie told me about how her faith is helping her to cope with this looming, permanent loss.

Jacquie's fear is similar to that of another friend, whose biggest fear is losing, because of all the losses she has experienced in life. She lost her husband, to whom she was married for thirty-seven years. She lost her retirement investments during a market downturn. She lost her personal information through identity theft. She's afraid of losing her mom, who at the time was seventy-nine years old. She lost a job that she loved. She continued to say, "The greatest loss of my life, was fertility. I did not get to be a mother. My husband didn't get to be a daddy."

For some of us, as losses such as these pile up, pessimism could easily take over, in anticipation of the next loss. With that anticipation comes the fear of losing. To cope with all these, my friend said, "I pray. I cry. I pray and cry and ask why. Then I wipe the tears, try to smile, and think of all the blessings in my life, and keep going on with my day." That's a very brave and courageous woman, for whom I have a lot of respect. Instead of allowing her losses to weigh her down, she chose instead to focus on her gains.

Nair's greatest fear was losing her children. She wrote to tell me, "After my mother and my grandmother passed, I felt adrift, like the anchors in my life were gone. I felt like the safe place that I could always go back to was no longer there. So, my children represent the future, the reason for me to keep going, the continuation of the unconditional love that I had from the beautiful women that raised me."[13] To overcome this fear, Nair also relies on her faith. She said, "I ask God to replace my fear with faith, and I reassure myself that God is watching over my children."

Yet another person fears the loss of an opportunity. This person said to me, "Any opportunity given has timing associated with it. When one does not invest the time well to explore the opportunity, one has nothing to gain but failure."

The fear of losing his job is Samuel's greatest fear.[14] This is a common fear for many people, especially if you live in a part of the world, where securing another job quickly doesn't come that easily. For Rick, it's the fear of losing his health, becoming ill, and not being able to recover or pay for his care.[15] To handle this, he became proactive in eating and staying healthy. Another person told me his greatest fear was mental incapacitation – losing his rational ability and aptitude. He said, "Working in healthcare, I have seen many lives come to an end in an empty shell that was once a vibrant life. I don't want to become a burden to my family." To cope with this, he said, "I seek solace in my relationship with God, knowing first and foremost that He is good."

While another friend, Kevin has made efforts to not be fearful (and has been mostly successful with it), he told me, "One thing that does create fear for me somewhat consistently is the fear of not having enough money to meet my obligations and live comfortably."[16] He said this fear became more prevalent after his divorce and being laid off from a job in a market that did not have a lot of openings. Ultimately, he made the decision to start his own business, and the success of that business has relieved many of his concerns.

For some us, the fear could be about our purpose in life. I'm going to come clean here and say that this is one thing I wrestle with frequently. I always ask myself, "Is what I'm doing God's will for me? Am I doing what I'm supposed to be doing? What if my purpose in life is different from what I'm doing?" Mary, another good friend seems to share this fear. She wrote to tell me that her greatest fear is not living out the will that God has for her life. She asks herself, "What if my fear gets in the way? What if I say 'yes' to the wrong opportunities? What if I say 'no' to a God-given opportunity because of my own insecurities? What if I let my own comforts get in the way of God's desire for my life?" That's a lot of "what ifs," and many of us struggle with similar questions on a daily basis.

To cope with this constant barrage of questions, Mary said,

> I focus on seeking wisdom from the Bible instead of my own desires. I present opportunities and ideas to God in prayer. I ask that my eyes be blindfolded from opportunities I am not to take, and that blinders are taken off for the opportunities I am to grasp onto. Then I place my trust in Him. I trust that I am exactly where I am supposed to be right at this moment. Every day I work on finding comfort through His guidance and the relationships in my life. I'm becoming more aware of "coincidences" that occur in my life and the way God speaks to me through others. I continue to focus on growing and investing in personal development and praying daily that God will use my talents and strengths for His purposes.[17]

That is so awesome! We can learn a lot from this amazing woman.

As we see all of these fears on display, it seems to me as if most of them have a foundation in how they make us look – either to ourselves or to others. While we may not consciously see our fears in the context of how they make us look, I think that's clearly what's happening in our subconscious. We fear losing our health or mental capacity because it makes us look helpless and dependent on others. We fear failure or not being able to meet our obligations because it makes us look weak and impotent. We fear losing people that are dear to us because it makes us look and feel as if we don't have love or caring people around us. Thus, many of our fears seem to stem from how they make us look to ourselves and to others. Some of them also come from our desire to be in control of every situation we're in.

For example, with a lot of people, the fear of public speaking is ranked as the number one fear. But if you take a closer look, the real fear is *not* in standing up in front of people and moving your lips while engaging your vocal cords in such a way that they form words that other people can hear and understand. Is it? All of us do that very well when we're surrounded by people with whom we're familiar. We speak boldly in the company of family and friends. Some of us do it loudly and excitedly when we are with people we know well. So, the issue is not with speaking publicly.

The real fear is in making ourselves look stupid and incompetent in front of others, especially those who don't know us that well. And some of the reasons for the fear don't even make sense! When I was active in Toastmasters, I have heard some of the most ridiculous reasons behind the fear of public speaking. Here are some of the real fears people have shared with me about standing to speak in front of others:

> What if the shape of my mouth as I speak doesn't look good?
>
> They could be staring at the mole on my face!
>
> They will make fun of my southern accent!
>
> They can see me shaking from anxiety!

I'm honestly not making this up! These were actual reasons that I personally heard. Every one of these come down to the fact that we don't want to look bad to others. We value others' opinions about us, so we don't want to do anything to jeopardize that. That's the genuine reason for this fear.

Early in my career as an engineer, I did not speak much in team meetings because I was afraid of saying the wrong thing. First of all, as an introvert, I naturally don't like to talk unless I have to. And when I feel the need to say something, I didn't want to look stupid in the presence of the more experienced engineers I was working with. Some around me chalked it up to my personality. "He's just a quiet person," they would say. While that may be true, I later discovered, with some reflection, that this wasn't the only reason I was quiet in those days. I was simply afraid of being seen as stupid or unintelligent. I was afraid that my contributions in those meetings would either be rejected or not seen as valuable.

It was much later that I came to understand that the fear of rejection is one fear that many of us deal with. While this fear can manifest itself in different ways, it's in most of us. That's because we are wired to want to belong. We desire to be loved and admired by others. The desire may be stronger in some of us when compared to others, but it's there in all of us. I've heard some people say, "I don't care what anybody thinks about me!" I think that's a big lie! I believe that is the way we like to communicate our independence and show to others that we're not vulnerable.

The truth is that no one likes being seen in a critical way. We don't want to experience the hurt and pain that comes from people's negative perception of us. We're anxious about being alone, isolated or cut off from others. And this rejection speaks volumes to us about our self-worth. More importantly, most of our fears tend to be the result of our need to protect and preserve our high view *The real fear of public speaking is in making ourselves look stupid in front of others.* of our own importance. As a result, we develop coping mechanisms to handle them. For me, it was to refrain from speaking, even when I should have. For others, it may be speaking out of turn – saying something when they should have kept their mouths shut. We develop different ways to cope, depending on our personalities. More importantly, we develop ways to cope because of how what we fear makes us look to ourselves or to those around us. We develop ways to cope because fear threatens our self-worth.

Imagine what will happen when we come to the realization of

the roots of our fears and then choose to not allow this to take over our lives. But that choice must be a deliberate one. It has to be intentional for us to overcome the fear. I don't know what you believe in, but I believe in God. My faith in God helps me overcome all my fears because I know who I am in Him. The same is true for many others. You can see this from some of the comments I've already shared with you, from others about how they deal with their fears. Swiss philosopher, Henri-Frédéric Amiel said, "It is not what he had, or even what he does which expresses the worth of a man, but what he is." As for me, when I put my trust in God and I give Him all my anxieties, worries, concerns, and fears, He gives me peace of mind. He also gives me the wisdom to know what I need to do, if there are things that I can do to alleviate those fears and concerns.

Ego and Self-Worth
Since fear threatens our self-worth, we try to protect ourselves from this threat. To deal with the fear, we put on something: a protection, such as an armor or a shield as a defense against the perceived danger that comes from the phobia. In my case, my shield was not speaking up in meetings. I thought, "If I don't say anything, I won't look stupid, right?" This was true even when I thought I had better ideas than what was being discussed. On many occasions, someone else would later say what I was thinking, and I would beat myself up for not speaking up when I had the chance. But that was the price I paid for the fear that my ideas might not be good enough and would be rejected.

One armor or shield that some of us use against the fear of rejection is ego. Author Rob White describes ego as the false version of yourself that you create in order to protect yourself so that no one could harm the real you. He said, "You were saying to the world, 'It's not the real me that you are scolding – it's a false version of me … ha ha to you.'" Eckhart Tolle calls ego "the voice in the head." It's who you think you are and not who you really are.

The ego that we use in dealing with the fear of rejection can show up in different ways. For example, ego can present itself in condescending behavior towards others. When you look down on others, you're subconsciously pulling yourself up, portraying yourself as better than them. You put them in their place before they have the chance to reject you. Other times, the ego shows up in wanting to belong and go along with an idea that you know is not a good one.

In 2003, when my family was still living in St. Charles, a suburb of St. Louis Missouri, I heard a story on the local evening news that still gives me shivers anytime I remember it. It was about a group of teenagers. Some of them were playing and riding around their neighborhood on skateboards while attending a church carnival. After a while they got bored and decided to try something else.

It is not what he had, or even what he does which expresses the worth of a man, but what he is.
Henri-Frédéric Amiel

One of them grabbed his skateboard and whacked his own head with it. He then boasted to his friends about how tough his skull was. After a few moments, they were all whacking their own heads with their skateboards. Soon, one of them decided it was time to raise the stakes. Instead of hitting their own heads, it was time for someone else to do it. So, he gave his skateboard to one of the other boys and told him to summon all his strength while hitting him on the head. He wanted to show others that his head could withstand whatever force any one of them could muster. His friend obliged. The victim immediately crumbled to the ground. Four days later, he died from the resulting head injury after being removed from life support. The boy who hit him in the head was charged with involuntary manslaughter.

Anytime I remember this fatal incident, my heart still goes out to the families of both boys, which is probably the reason I can still recall the story more than fifteen years later. While the story did not elaborate further, and I didn't know any more than what was reported on the local news at the time, here's my take on this.

It is highly probable that none of these boys gave much thought to their actions and the potentially fatal consequences before the eventual outcome. However, I'm willing to bet that there's at least one of those boys who must have had a few second thoughts about what was going on. It's likely he must have thought that this was not a good idea, but he did not say anything because of the fear of rejection – being made fun of and called "chicken" by his friends. He probably decided to shield his fear with a false bravado and go along with the others. The result was a family changed forever as they mourn the loss of their child. And another family changed forever because of their child being charged with involuntary manslaughter. Also, their friends who were present will always live with the regret of what happened that evening.

Therefore, when next you see someone behaving in a manner that seems egocentric and self-centered to you, try to look beyond the façade and the disguise of the behavior. There's probably an underlying fear lurking under the cover of what you see; a fear that's being covered up with the behavior you're seeing – fear that ultimately connects to how that person sees themselves and their own importance.

What You Get
The manner in which you and I communicate reveals a lot about how we see our own level of importance. Whether it's in the words you speak or how you express yourself on social media platforms, humility and arrogance are apparent to those on the receiving end of your communications. Even with casual conversations, I've come across people who seems to turn around every discussion to be about them.

Ask yourself, "When I speak, am I talking about you or am I talking about me? Is the focus of my speech on me and what I've got to do or am I interested in you and how you're doing? When I talk about me, what percentage of that is around the areas that I need to grow, as opposed to talking about my accomplishments?"[23] Humble people do not talk much about themselves, especially if doing so shines a positive light on them and what they have accomplished. They talk about others instead, and shine the light on them.

What we say and how we express it either shows humility or the lack of it. When you and I begin to pay attention to our expressions, whether they are vocal, written or in any other form, we receive the benefits that come from the humility inherent in those expressions. Here are two major benefits of being humble in how you express yourself:

- You build bridges and connections with people, instead of creating gaps between you and them. The connections you build can create an array of opportunities for you.

- It boosts your image with others when you overcome your fears and do those things that you think make you look less than you actually are. I've discovered that when we intentionally exhibit areas of short-coming to others, it endears us to them. It connects us to them. They feel comfortable around us. It makes us human.

What You Can Do
If you're given to boasting about who you are or what you have accomplished, whether verbally or through other means, it's probably valuable for you to know that you're not fooling most people. It's fairly easy to spot. What you actually get is the opposite of your desire to be appreciated or celebrated. It turns people off. Here are some things that can help.

1. Ask people who know you well if they think you're prone to excessive boasting. Find out from them about how they feel anytime they see the behavior in you. Be true to yourself and ensure you really want to know. They will tell you if they sense that you're honest. Don't get upset nor be defensive about the responses you get. Do not shoot the messenger!

2. From the responses you receive, take a closer look at why you tend to exhibit those behaviors. Think about what you're trying to cover up. Is there a fear lurking somewhere there?

3. Take a moment to think about what you need to do. Come up with strategies that you can use to prevent these behaviors in the future. Are there specific

situations that bring out the bravado in you? Pay attention to those conditions and make a conscious effort to overcome them.

4.   Let the people from whom you sought feedback know that you're working on changing. You can ask them to point out anytime they see you exhibit the behavior from now on. Also, tell them to let you know when they see improvements.

5.   What fears do you have? What are you afraid of?

6.   Take time to think about the root of (or the reasons behind) your fears. Does it have anything to do with how you look to others? Does it attack your self-worth?

7.   What opportunities for growth does this afford you? What can you do to begin confronting this fear?

Communicating the right things in the right way and at the right time helps us to exhibit humility. The same goes for having the right consideration for other people. That is next.

CHAPTER 5
THE POWER OF RESPECT

There is no respect for others
without humility in one's self.
                    – Henri-Frédéric Amiel

W hile flying back home to the United States from
        Singapore in August 2014, I had a connecting flight
        through Narita International Airport in Tokyo. Until
that time, I had never been to Japan. As a result, I wanted to make
the best use of my three-hour layover to see as much as I could.
Since I couldn't leave the airport, I took advantage of the array of
floor-to-ceiling windows throughout the terminal.

As I wandered around, I noticed a Japanese family of four –
father, mother, boy, and girl. The boy must have been around ten
years old. I saw him talking excitedly to his parents while pointing
to another person close by. To my surprise, the mom slapped the
boy's hand, pulling it down and warning him harshly. Of course,
I did not understand what either of them said, but their body
languages said it all. Still, I could not comprehend what the boy
said that warranted the stern rebuke from his mother. It wasn't
until a few years later when I discovered that it probably had
nothing to do with what the boy said. It was most likely his
gesture.

The act of pointing at people is considered rude in the Japanese culture. It shows disrespect. Instead of using a finger to point, they would gently wave their hand with the palm facing up, at whoever it is they're referring to. In many other parts of the world, we can point to people willy-nilly, and it's not considered rude. So, it seems what one culture considers rude, another may deem acceptable. Respect, when seen from this perspective, seems to be relative. It depends on the culture.

Most African cultures value respect. Even so, the manner in which respect is demonstrated, differs greatly across cultures. For the Nigerian *Yoruba* culture in which I grew up, respect is very important. In fact, I think the typical *Yoruba* person elevates respect higher than many of the other ethnic groups in Nigeria. It's very important to us, and it shows up in different ways. For example, we don't call our older siblings by their first names. There are other ethnic groups in Nigeria who call their older siblings by their first names. To the Yoruba person, that's a huge sign of disrespect. If, as a child, you call someone older than you by their first name, that name gets slapped from your mouth very quickly before it makes its complete exit from your vocal cords. You quickly learn to refer to your older siblings as *bù'ọdá mi* (my brother), *sìstá mi* (my sister) or the more gender-neutral *ẹgbọn mi* (my older one). In general, for most African cultures, respect typically flows from the younger to the older, from those being led to the leader.

The kind of respect I've described so far has its origin in cultures. I want to make it clear that the respect I'll be referring to in the rest of this chapter, is **not** this type that is rooted in cultures. That's because cultures differ. And because cultures differ, the way respect is shown will also be different. As I mentioned before, what one culture sees as rude and unacceptable, another culture may have no problems with it. For example, I also learned a while ago that in Japan, giving tips at restaurants can be seen as rude and insulting, while it's perfectly acceptable and even expected in most western cultures. I'm sure you can find anecdotes of what respect looks like from the perspective of the culture in which you were raised or currently live.

For our context in this book, I define *respect* as "the act of giving consideration to others." This definition will be applicable

The Power of Respect

irrespective of culture. The concept will become clear as we take a look at how showing respect for others can help us learn to be humble.

Clue-less or Care-less

It was an early morning flight out of San Francisco International Airport. I was still tired and sleepy from having to wake up at 3 o'clock in the middle of the night to get ready for my trip back home that Friday morning. Boarding for my flight started just before 5:30 am.

I was able to board early. Once in the airplane, I took my seat and began people-watching as many of us are inclined to do – observing as other passengers came on board. With their faces up, they scanned the labels on the overhead panels, looking for their seat assignments. Then I saw him.

He stood just across from me in the aisle. I don't know his name, but let's call him Fred. After putting his duffel bag in one of the overhead compartments, Fred took his time going through the motions of taking off his winter jacket and gloves. He followed this by folding them very slowly and meticulously before finally stowing them on top of his duffel bag. As I watched him, it was as if everything was happening in slow-motion.

All the while, he was standing in the aisle, and a long line had formed behind him. He seemed to be completely oblivious to the announcement by one of flight attendants that people should find their seats quickly and move away from the aisle. Or maybe he was just ignoring it. Other passengers were trying to get to their seats, but traffic was at a standstill because of Fred. I noticed that the gentleman at the head of that line had a stern look on his face; but he said nothing. He was standing behind Fred, waiting impatiently. With his back turned, Fred could not see this man, but I could see his face as clear as day. I could tell that he was fuming. I was actually afraid that he was about to blow a gasket. His angry gaze bore holes on the back of Fred's head, but our friend seemed to be completely unaware of what was going on behind him.

What one culture considers rude, another may deem acceptable.

89

Absolutely clueless as to what had just happened, Fred eventually completed his stowing ritual and took his seat. Then the traffic started moving again.

Just like Fred, some of us are completely unaware of how our behaviors come across to others. Many times, such obliviousness tends to betray our sense of self-importance. We fail to see the impact of what we do on others. When that happens, it's either one of two things:

1. We're completely clueless as to how our behavior affects those around us.

2. We know the effects of our behavior on others, but we just don't care.

Without any words, Fred was either saying to the other passengers behind him:

"This is my world. I'm the only one in it."

OR

"I got here first. I'll take my time to do all that I need to do. I could care less about how this affects you."

I could easily tell that the guy behind Fred wasn't at all pleased with what was going on. His facial expression and body language told the whole story. In fact, at one time, I was afraid that he would do something drastic, such as push Fred into one of the seats or give him a serious tongue-lashing. Thankfully, he did neither.

Even though that man did nothing to express his displeasure, don't count on everyone to show a similar restraint. Remi[1] wrote to tell me about a very similar experience she had during one of her overseas travels. In her case, she was the one right behind this clueless fellow traveler. After a few moments of waiting, she couldn't take it anymore – she told the man to make way for her to get to her seat. As she moved past him, all she could think about was that this person must be a very selfish individual who had no

The Power of Respect

regard for how his behavior affected others.

I'm also reminded of another encounter at a McDonald's fast-food restaurant many years ago. I was in the line, waiting to order a *Happy Meal* for my daughter when she was little. She loved the Happy Meals because of the tiny promotional toys that came with each meal. The line was longer than usual that day, probably because the lady at the front of the line was taking her time to order. I mean, she was really taking her time. To the chagrin of those patiently waiting in line behind her, she would make a choice from the menu, and then change her mind. Then she would select another item and change it again seconds later. This menu-item select-and-reject game she was playing seemed to go on forever. After what seemed like an eternity to those of us behind her in the line, her friend tried to hurry her along. She told her there were other people waiting in line to place orders. Her response was an impatient remark that people should wait for their turns, just as she had waited for hers. "It's my turn to order, and I'll take as much time as I need," was her irritated reply. Her friend quickly backed off and kept quiet.

Some of us are completely oblivious to how our behaviors sometimes betray our sense of self-importance.

As I noted moments ago, some people may not realize the impact of their behavior on others, but I don't think that was the case with this lady at McDonald's. From what I saw, she just didn't care! I think that is a far worse scenario than just being oblivious. It involves a complete lack of humility that reveals itself in not showing respect for people and in having a low consideration of others. In other words, this lady was saying to the rest of us on that line, "I'm more important than you. My time is more valuable than yours. I don't care about how this affects you. I'll do what I need to do, I'll take my time doing it, and there's nary a thing you can do about it!"

Here's something important that I've found out about this particular attitude. For those who exhibit this behavior, it doesn't show up in just a specific area. It rears its ugly head in almost every aspect of their lives. Unfortunately, true to their oblivious or "don't care" nature, they are either unaware or don't give a hoot about how this is negatively impacting their success in life. The repercussions can be felt in both their personal and business endeavors.

Taking all the time you want, to do something without any regard to how that's affecting others may cause you to be forever engaging in a futile chase of success for the rest of your life. That's because people will quickly realize that they cannot depend on you. As a result, you will always be lacking much needed help. No one wants to give assistance to someone who's always wasting their time. Even when you're prepared to pay for their services, you will quickly discover that not many people are willing to work with someone who has no respect for them or their time. If there's no one to help you, success in both your personal life and professional goals will elude you. That was the experience that Rebecca had.

Rebecca had a music business, which included giving piano lessons. She told me about an experience that left her perplexed and frustrated. Here's what she said:

> There are times when I must travel to the student's location, sometimes during rush hour traffic. What this means is that, on these trips, I'm on the road, driving each way for forty-five minutes. On arrival, there are times when the student would not show up for their lessons in their own home!!! Other times, they have made no attempts to practice what I taught them between lessons. In the worst cases, when I bring up the importance of practicing what they've learned to their attention, they would tell me that they should not have to practice, and that I need to teach them or they'll not pay me. They said they shouldn't have to practice since the act of practicing does not actually teach them anything; it's just busy work. They would say that if I'm such a good teacher, they should understand the music after I've taught them.

The Power of Respect

Does this attitude sound ridiculous to you as it does to me? Rebecca continued,

> This attitude makes me very angry. While I'm not responsible for how they spend their time, having to teach them the same lesson over and over again shows that they have no respect for my time. I bring enormous value to each student. Even the fact that I travel to them is a service that is rarely provided by other teachers. Because of this, I have fired several students. I don't miss them![2]

Rebecca shared this incident with me because I asked about her experience with behaviors that do not respect others people's time. It's difficult for me to get over the arrogance in this person's attitude towards practicing what they're being taught. This was someone who could not grasp the importance of using repetitive practice to grow and hone the skills they want to develop. With their sense of self-importance, they put the blame on the teacher – "If you're a good enough teacher, I shouldn't have to practice playing the music for me to know how to play it well!" This is an attitude that is completely devoid of reality. That is an outlook that will destroy success in every area of life.

As you and I continue to wonder about how clueless this person is, let's look inward for a moment. That's because we may be equally oblivious in one or more areas of our lives. Just as this person's cluelessness was not glaring to them, yours may not be very obvious to you either. So, we need to ask ourselves, "In what way is my being oblivious betraying my sense of self-importance? How are these behaviors impacting those with whom I come into contact? How are these affecting the level of success I can achieve in life?"

These questions will help us get a glimpse of how people with whom we interact see our behaviors. They help you truly see you.

Do You See You?
At work, Oliver had a habit of arriving late for almost every meeting. His tardiness ranged anywhere from five to thirty

minutes. Sometimes, he wouldn't even show up at all. Each time this happened, he would apologize profusely for being late. After a while, he started to notice something different each time he arrived late to a meeting. Nobody said anything to him, but the body language from members of his team started speaking volumes. He could tell that he was losing a lot of respect, so he decided to do something about it.

He began by asking a trusted member of his team. He knew Jill would tell him the truth, so he asked about her thoughts concerning what he had been observing lately during his meetings.

> **Oliver**: "Jill, can you tell me what's going on? Over the last few weeks, I've noticed a change within the team anytime I arrive for our weekly meeting. What am I missing?"
>
> **Jill**: "What do you mean? What kind of change have you noticed?"
>
> **Oliver**: "Honestly, I can't really put my finger on it, but I know that something's wrong. Lately, I can feel the change in the energy within the room whenever I arrive at each meeting."
>
> **Jill**: "Well, I think it's because you're always late for every meeting."
>
> **Oliver**: "Oh that! You know how busy I am, don't you? For each meeting, I have to practically run from my prior meeting in Building 1 to Building 9. And they're back-to-back on my calendar. What can I do?"
>
> **Jill**: "I know that you're busy, and you always have a valid reason for not being on time. But after a while, those reasons just come across as excuses."
>
> **Oliver**: "Really?! That's what it looks like?"
>
> **Jill**: "Yes, it is. In fact, a few weeks ago, we started a weekly bet about what excuse you'd

come up with, as we wait for your arrival. That wager may be responsible for the change you observed on the team on arrival each time."

Oliver: "Wow!"

Jill: "I've also noticed that many times, you arrive out of breath because you were either running or walking fast to the meeting. That seems to always give the impression that you are disorganized."

Oliver: "I had no idea! Thank you for being candid with me about this.

This conversation was an eye-opening experience for Oliver. If members of his own team saw him this way, he wondered how others, who do not know him as well, were seeing him. He decided that he had to do something about it.

And he did.

For the next meeting, he arrived early, which shocked most members of his team. He then addressed the issue with them. He apologized for being late in the past. He also promised to pay more attention to planning his meetings so that there are breaks between them that will allow him time to end one meeting and still be on time for the next.

He who knows the universe and does not know himself knows nothing.
Jean De La Fontaine

Those of us who are like Oliver tend not to see ourselves the way others see us. It's almost as if we're blind to our environment. We don't see the way our behaviors come across to those around us and the potential impact of those behaviors on our relationships. We all have different ways of interacting with our environment and processing the information that we receive. When you become aware of the differences between how you see your interactions and how others perceive the same interactions, you begin to get a solid foundation upon which you can build strong, effective, and lasting relationships. This is a component of self-awareness, and it has a very strong link to humility. How you see yourself and your behaviors will determine how you express yourself to others.

Unfortunately, as it was the case with Oliver, many who show up late (or don't show up at all) for agreed appointments do not realize the impact and depth of what they're communicating to others by those actions. Here are some of the words that people used to express how they felt when someone was late or stood them up:

bad.[3]	disappointed.[4]	disrespected.[4,6,11]
furious![5]	used![5]	devalued.[6]
irritated.[7,9]	angry.[8]	frustrated.[8,9]
resentful.[9]	unhappy.[10]	upset.[8,11]
very, very, displeased![12]		

Consider this: how would you feel if someone described the effect of your actions (or inactions) on them with one or more of these words? Take a moment to let that sink in. And there are probably some who will say, "I don't care what others think!" Hold that thought; we will discuss this further in a moment. But whether you care or not, the effects of your behaviors on others can go a long way in shaping their perceptions about who you are. This could in turn determine the extent of their willingness to cooperate with you or help you when you really need it.

With high self-awareness, we begin to understand ourselves better – our tendencies and preferences. We also gain insight into the reasons we behave the way we do and why we respond to things the way we respond to them. In addition, we start to understand how others may be different from us and how our tendencies and preferences may not be the same as theirs. Also, self-awareness involves understanding how our behaviors come across to other people and the impact of our actions on them.

As you and I begin to pay attention to how our behaviors affect other people, our level of self-awareness begins to increase. When that happens, we can take active steps to behave towards others in ways that value and respect them. As a result, we move away from self-serving behaviors that seem to elevate our view of our own

The Power of Respect

importance. We move closer to thinking about others and caring for them.

Do You Care?

Several years ago, a colleague and I were walking through an underground link on the campus of the company we were both working with at that time. The link connected all the buildings on the campus; the walls and floors were built with red, beautiful bricks. The entire link was usually clean, spotless and sparkling.

After a few moments as we walked, we suddenly stumbled upon a crumpled piece of paper lying innocuously on the brick floor. It definitely looked out of place. As we walked pass it, my friend bent down and picked it up. He said nothing about it, and neither did I. We just continued with our conversation. When we got to the next building and passed by the coffee machine, he dropped the paper in the trash bin.

Why do you think my colleague stopped to pick up the wrinkled piece of paper? And why do you think others before us passed by the same piece of paper and never bothered to pick it up? How about the person who dropped it? The entire area was clean, except for the crumpled paper. Who dropped it? More importantly, why did they drop it without any regard for how clean the place was? Was it dropped intentionally? Or maybe it was an accidental drop.

All of these questions can be answered easily when you consider something emotional intelligence experts call *Social Responsibility*. It is defined as one's willingness to contribute to society, to one's social groups, and generally to the welfare of others. It also involves acting responsibly, having social consciousness, and showing concern for the greater community. In short, it's looking out for others, and doing things that benefit other people instead of engaging in acts that are detrimental to them. Although I didn't tell my colleague at that time, I knew he was one of the more socially responsible ones amongst us.

Compare this behavior with that in an old high school video that I came across recently. In the short clip, this guy was giving a speech while running for class president as a senior in high school. In the video, he was captured asking the student body in his high school,

> "Am I the only one who is sick and tired of being told to pick up my trash when we have plenty of janitors who are paid to do it for us?!"[13]

What a sharp contrast this is! Here was my colleague, willing to pick up *someone else's* trash. And another person who's "sick and tired of being told" to pick up *his own* trash! Which one are you? Do you litter and expect others to pick up after you? Or are you the type that picks up after other people. This behavior is just one of many that shows how much consideration you show for others in general.

Showing consideration for others is a sign of respect. It's a sign of respect that flows from a humble heart. When you consider others and how they are affected in everything that you do, you attract a lot of goodwill from them. Anytime you think there's a job that's beneath you, what you're really saying is that there are people who are beneath you. And you expect those who are beneath you to do the job that's beneath you. What that means is that you have no respect for such people. Your view of your own importance is so high that

When you think there's a job that's beneath you, you have no respect for the people doing that job.

it trumps everything else. How we treat people because of what they do can eventually extend to how we treat what is theirs.

Don't Do to Others

When we show consideration for others, it reflects not just in how we treat them, but also in how we handle what belongs to them. This reminds me of something that happened almost twenty years ago.

Victor and Pamela were a middle-class husband and wife couple. They lived in one of America's mid-western states. One day, their only car broke down, and it was taking a while to get it fixed. Because they live in the suburb of a major city in middle of the country that lacked public transportation, their day-to-day activities were impacted. It became suddenly difficult for them to do the things they were accustomed to, such as taking the kids to school, running errands or even getting rides to their jobs. To get through each day, they had to rely mostly on the generosity of their neighbors and friends, who took turns lending them a vehicle to use for a few hours on most days.

After this had gone on for about two weeks, another couple that was one of their closest friends called them with a proposal. Instead of them having to call different people each day to drop their children at school or give them a ride to work, Simon and Jenny offered them one of their own two vehicles on a permanent basis for a short period of time.

Simon told Victor, "Since Jenny doesn't use her car all the time, why don't you take it, and use it for the one or two weeks that your car is being fixed. Whenever she needs a car, I can coordinate my schedule with hers, so she can use my car." Victor and Pamela were excited and thankful. They gladly took the car, and it was of great help to them.

When the car was returned one week later, it had a cracked windshield and an extra 2,000 miles on it. They were thankful, but there was no comment about what happened to the windshield. Simon couldn't believe it. 2,000 miles! Where did they drive it to? Timbuktu?! That's twice the number of miles he puts on his car in a whole month! And what about the windshield? He was at least expecting an attempt to explain how the crack happened, but none came. He wanted to ask Victor, but his wife persuaded him not to, in order to preserve their friendship. The experience left such a sour taste in Simon's mouth that he quietly decided not to offer such help in the future.

It's amazing to me to see how many of us don't take extra care when we use other people's property. We callously handle things that belong to others as if we're at war with them. Some even justify such treatment, especially if they had paid for the opportunity to use the items – such as with a rental car. Their attitude seems to be, "I paid for it! I can use it however I want!" For example, I've heard some horror stories about what some people do in their rental cars. Some of them are returned with so much garbage and other unimaginable things that it gives you pause – from drugs to firearms, from gasoline (left inside the vehicle for a day or two to marinate) to dirty diapers (that have been stewing overnight). They never give consideration to the fact that all of these items would have to be cleaned up by real human beings. Yes, they may be paid to do the cleaning, but do you have to make their jobs extra difficult? It's so easy to not think of them since they're faceless to you. You simply don't care because you don't know them.

You're probably protesting right now. You could be thinking, "I don't do all those terrible things to others' property! I treat others' stuff just like I would treat mine." Okay, I'll give you that, but I want you to consider something for a moment. You may not be doing those exact same things I described, but are you making efforts to treat them with extra care simply because they're not yours? Some of us employ the golden rule, to do to others as you would have them do to you; which seems fair to most people. You may say that you use these items as you would use yours. But how do you know if the way you're using them is the way the owner would like them to be used? Just think about that for a moment.

If, for example, I have formed the habit of not using my house, my car and my appliances with carefulness, that's likely the same way I would use them if I were to borrow these from others. What happens if the owner sees the way I use their items, and they don't like it? If they were borrowed, what would prevent them from asking me to return the items even when I still have need for them? I have seen this happen a few times. The owner feigns an immediate need for their property and wants it back. Sometimes, they may not be that bold to demand it back right away, but they will take note for the future. Once returned, they know that there's no way they're lending *any* of their property to you ever again. You end up being the loser, just because you don't give consideration to others and what belongs to them. You have burned that bridge.

Instead of burning bridges, we should be building them. As we pay attention to giving consideration to others, it's also helpful to give extra consideration to their property whenever we have the privilege of being temporary custodians of such. In other instances, we can also become a temporary custodian of something that belongs to others by protecting them from a ditch they're about to fall into, even when they don't realize it.

At the Parking Meter

One day during the summer of 2016, I was feeding coins into a parking meter in downtown Omaha, Nebraska just after arriving for a lunch meeting. As I waited for the rusty machine to reflect my payment, and note how long I could park there, I heard a voice behind me.

> "Sir, I'm not sure you know, but they will give you a ticket for parking like that."

I turned around to see who it was. A young lady who was passing by with three of her friends smiled at me. I glanced at my car, saw nothing wrong with my parking and then turned to her.

> "What do you mean? How should I have parked?"

> "In these parking spaces around here, you have to park backwards," she responded.

> "Oh, really?! I didn't know. I'll re-park. Thank you!" was my reply as she walked past me.

And I did, once I saw that my payment was good for a two-hour period.

As I walked to my meeting that day, I reflected on what had just happened. Until that moment, I had never met the young lady who gave me the parking tip. But as she walked by, and saw me doing something that could result in a hefty parking ticket, she decided to speak up. I began to wonder what percentage of the population would have done what she did. I wondered if *I* would have done what she did!

Yes, I try to lend a helping hand as much as I could. Yet, it's very likely that I would have just walked by and not say anything if I were in her shoes. But she didn't do that. And in the process, she saved me from what could have been a huge parking fine.

Now, what would have been the reason for me to not speak up when I see someone that's obviously about to get in trouble? Could it be because I don't care enough? While that may be true for some, I don't think that's the case for most of us.

I realized that I probably would not have said anything simply because I may not have been paying attention to what was going on around me. I could be looking at the person and not really be seeing them. Their actions would be right in my face, but my brain may not be computing what the consequences would be for them. As a result, I may not have spoken up.

This is often what happens with many of us. We go about our daily activities, just letting life pass us by, clueless as to what's happening around us. I think this attitude is actually getting worse with our current culture of walking around, hunched over as we stare into, and fiddle with our smart phones. In the process, we miss countless opportunities – chances to do something for someone; to add value to others. Just imagine the opportunities you will find if you actually go around looking for ways to do something to help another person! There will be plenty to find. And when you find one, you will be ready to do something about it. That is living and acting with intentionality.

> *The most persistent and urgent question of life is 'what are you doing for others?'*
> Martin Luther King, Jr.

A few years ago, I was in a conference in Orlando, Florida where I heard leadership guru, John C. Maxwell speak about one of his grandchildren. The boy woke up one day, and decided that he would look for opportunities to open doors for others. By noon of that same day, he had opened doors for more than forty people. Forty doors opened! Imagine that! Do you think it would have happened if he hadn't made up his mind to do that as he got up that morning? I don't think so!

When with the dawn of each day, you purpose in your heart to add value to others, and you go everywhere with that resolve in mind, a myriad of opportunities will be available for you to do so.

The Power of Respect

As you act on these, you're spreading goodwill. In the process, you feel good about yourself and you get boosts of positive energy to get more done. You become more productive. And it may even lead to doors being opened to a whole new world for you. There's a line in a poem by Edwin Markham that goes: *"All that we send into the lives of others comes back into our own."*

So, I ask: do you wake up each day thinking of who you can help, serve, or do something for? And it need not be something special or earth-shattering. It could be as simple as holding doors open for others as your walk through them. It could be a courteous smile or a kind word to someone that needs encouragement. When you go around looking for opportunities to do something good for someone, you're not focused on yourself. Your focus is on others. In those moments, you don't have a high view of your own importance.

Once you've decided on what to do, you need to be intentional about following through with specific actions on the opportunities that you encounter. Don't just wander around letting life happen to you. Make the choice to be observant to what's happening around you, and take action to help others. One good outcome from this is that you will be happier. All kinds of research have been done that shows that when you lend a helping hand to others, you also benefit from the resulting boost of positive emotions.

Another wonderful outcome of this behavior is that you become more empathetic when you see actions that would otherwise have made you judgmental. With the positive thoughts stemming from empathy replacing the negatives ones that come from condemning, you begin to live a much happier life. The choice is yours, and you can start today.

When you live an intentional life, you can make a difference in the lives of people that you come across each day. That daily difference shows a level of respect for others – respect that says you don't see yourself as more important than they are. And that difference can go a long way in making someone's day a special one, just like that young lady did for me at the parking meter.

The Servant Leader

By definition, a servant is humble. The position of a servant has inherent humility built into it. At least, it's supposed to. And that's because to the servant, whoever they are serving is more important than they are. An arrogant servant is an oxymoron. Since humility is focused on the importance of others, humble people usually serve other people. They go out of their way to help. They do that because they do not consider themselves as better or more important than others.

The phrase, "servant leadership" was coined by Robert K. Greenleaf in an essay he first published in 1970. Since then, this term has become very popular in business lingo to describe the type of leadership that focuses on helping those being led. For someone to be this type of leader, they must first respect and value the contributions of those who are being led. This means they do not have

There is a destiny which makes us brothers; none goes his way alone.
All that we send into the lives of others comes back into our own.
Poem by Edwin Markham

a high view of their own importance. Instead, they see their team members and their contributions as uniquely more important, so they put the needs of their team first and they use their leadership to motivate the team to perform at the highest level.

Servant-leaders are not power-hungry. They share power instead. That's because their primary goal is to serve – the serving comes first. It's called *servant-leader*, not *leader-servant*, for a reason. In his essay, Greenleaf declared that, "The servant-leader is servant first. It begins with the natural feeling that one wants to serve, to serve first. Then conscious choice brings one to aspire to lead."[14]

Because servant-leaders are servants first, they choose to serve first. That's their primary motivation. This creates in them, an internal drive to rally others and inspire them towards the goal of the service. They know that they have to bring others in, because they understand that the work is too great for them to accomplish alone. They see the importance of, and the value in others to get the work done. As a result, there's no servant-leader without seeing the importance of others and what they bring to the table. This shows respect. This is humility.

One of the major attributes of the servant-leader is that they seek opportunities to understand and help because of the value they see in others. I once read about the experience of an executive that perfectly illustrates this. Andre Zotoff was the Vice President & General Manager of the iconic Hotel Del Coronado resort in San Diego, California.[15] On this particular day, one of the servers in the resort was "off" in his performance and made a mistake with an order. Instead of apologizing and offering to fix it, he brushed it off and basically dismissed the guest's dissatisfaction. Later the same day, Andre received a complaint from the guest, asserting that they had never experienced such poor service in the more than twenty years they had been coming to the resort. She further stated

When the positive thoughts stemming from empathy begin to replace the negative ones that come from condemning, we begin to live a much happier life.

that as a result of the poor service at lunch, she had made the decision to never return and to hold future events elsewhere.

Losing such valuable, long-term guest was not what Andre wanted to hear. So, he called the server to his office, read the note from the guest and explained the situation. The server, visibly uncomfortable asked, "Are you going to write me up or fire me?" To his surprise, Andre responded, "Neither. Please have a seat and let's figure out how to fix this together." He asked the server what was going on. After a while, Andre determined that he was just having a difficult day. Together, they then wrote a note of apology to the guest, explaining how the server was having an off day and that there was no excuse for his actions and attitude. The letter was honest and sincere. And they delivered it to the guest that evening.

The next day, the server saw the guest in the hotel lobby. Most probably because of his experience with Andre the previous day, he walked over to the guest and personally apologized. They continued to speak and after a while, tears began to stream down the server's face. He felt horrible for having such a negative effect on the guest's experience and the organization that he was trusted to represent. As a result, the issue was resolved and the guest accepted his apology. She then booked her next stay before she left the resort.

If you were Andre, how would you have responded after receiving the guest's complaint? Most of us would have probably written the server up or fire him on the spot; especially since he showed no remorse even after being confronted. But that was not Andre's approach. Instead, he took the time to understand what was going on with him. He did this because he did not see the server as a worthless, dispensable worker that he could easily replace. He understood that we all have bad days on occasions, and he used the opportunity to coach and mentor him. It's very possible that because of Andre's kindness to him, this server became an excellent ambassador of the hotel brand. This was evident when he saw the guest the next day and took action without being prompted by anyone.

> *The servant-leader is servant first. It begins with the natural feeling that one wants to serve; to serve first.*
> Robert K. Greenleaf

Anytime you see the value in others, despite their shortcomings, and you behave towards them in ways that demonstrate that value, you make deposits in them. Some of these deposits can grow and accrue interest over time, eventually culminating in the same outlook that sees value in others. As you do this, you begin to spread a message of goodwill; a message not delivered in words, but with action. That's a message that seeks to elevate others, rather than demean them.

Lower for Higher
Did you hear about the feud that happened on an airplane the morning of November 28, 2013? That was the day of that year's Thanksgiving holiday in the United States. The details were posted on Twitter by one of the passengers on the plane, who stated that he exchanged increasingly hostile notes with a fellow passenger on the flight.

The tale of this dispute spread very rapidly, with the posts getting more than five million views within a very short time. Even the prestigious *New York Times* got involved, and posted a link to the story in its travel section blog. After the story had spread widely, Elan Gale, a television producer, who was the author of the Twitter posts, revealed that the entire story had been fabricated. But by that time, it had already become a huge news item.

In today's culture of social media saturation, there is so much competition for readers that many digital news outlets feel they do not have the time to fact-check their sources and the validity of stories before disseminating them. That's what happened to the New York Times with this story. No one wants to peddle stale news. Most major news outlets want to report on breaking news as it unfolds. As a result, some occasionally fall into the trap of reporting stories that are not worthy of being reported as news items.

Heard any juicy gossip lately? Just like the airplane faux feud, some stories tend to just take on a life of their own, relying on the passion of those who retell them. Before you know it, they turn into amazing tales that people cannot wait to share with others. In fact, I have seen some people argue passionately about the veracity of a story they heard from another source as if their very existence depended on it. They retell the stories with the same passion an eye-witness would have.

Behaviors similar to this happen quite frequently in our personal lives and relationships. We hear a story about someone, and we can't wait to tell somebody! It could be about a coworker, neighbor, friend or family member. The story becomes salacious when it's about something negative that they've done or got caught up in. Bad stories about someone travel faster than a mid-summer California wildfire. There are itching ears waiting to hear them, and we simply cannot wait to scratch those ears with tales that are either outright lies or end up being embellished.

Just imagine the thrill of finding out something scandalous about someone, whether real or imagined. Then, add to that the anticipation of sharing that information with somebody else. Many of us can barely wait to tell the story we heard or inferred, to another person. In many cases, this other person has nothing to do with the situation, and neither can they help with it. But we just have to tell them! We have to tell them because we naturally like the negatives about others.

We have a natural tendency to quickly believe the negative opinions and perspectives about others. Sometimes it doesn't matter how well we know the person, once we hear something unbecoming about them, we tend to discount all the good we know about them and immediately give credence to the negative. Other times, we may not know much about them, but we believe the bad stuff we hear about them even before there's any evidence to support it.

... some people argue passionately about the veracity of a story they heard from another source as if their very existence depends on it.

I remember in the mid-2000's when the news first broke that some players in Major League Baseball may have been using performance enhancing drugs. I was living in St. Louis, Missouri at the time, so it was newsworthy when one of the players named immediately when the news first broke, played for our beloved St. Louis Cardinals. Along with many of my colleagues, I was (and still am) a passionate Cardinals fan. The very first time we heard the news, I was surprised by how quickly one of my colleagues began casting aspersions on the named player, saying the steroids he had been taking were responsible for his high levels of performance. This was before any proof or evidence was even presented. Once the first person determined the guilt of this player, most of the others quickly agreed.

Why do we do this? Why do we quickly believe the negative about people with little or no evidence to support it? And why do we feel the need to share such negative opinions with people who have no business knowing about it? I see this happen more frequently when the targets are people who are either popular or admired by a lot of people. Once again, why do this?

I have a theory on the why, but this is not just my opinion. Dr. Melanie Green, a social psychologist at the University of North

The Power of Respect

Carolina, Chapel Hill, said that we do this because "we want to see something new, maybe escape our lives."[16] We desire a break from the normal and the mundane to experience something exciting. Negative and sensational stories about other people make this happen.

I believe another reason we do this is because it makes us feel better about ourselves. Just think about that for a moment. Can you recall a situation where you've gossiped about someone? (C'mon! You know you have!) Do you remember how you felt? It felt good, didn't it? In fact, it's better than good. You felt better! Better than the person you were gossiping about. Subconsciously, when you and I do this, here's what we're implying: "I'm not like that person! I'm way better than them!"

It almost seems as if we're just waiting in the wings, looking for the opportunity to take them down from their lofty pedestal. I think it's because of our natural tendency to want to elevate ourselves by degrading others. We pull ourselves up by pushing others down. We try to have a higher view of our own importance by lowering, demoting, demeaning and denigrating others. Otherwise, why would we quickly conclude that someone is guilty of what they've just been accused of before any evidence has been presented?

We make ourselves look better by making others look worse than we are. We make them look worse than they may actually be. We try to push someone lower in order to pull ourselves higher. We think we're better. And we do feel better, even if only for a moment. With gossip, we put into words, our low opinions and consideration of others. With humility, on the contrary, we deliberately take the focus off our own importance in order to pull others higher, to help them.

Those of us in leadership especially have the unique responsibility to help those we lead. Good leaders have the well-being and development of their team members as one of their primary goals. It takes humility to do this well. You have to know and respect the inherent value in that person to do this. Yes, you may need to discuss their growth opportunity with others who could help in this area, but it's not your business to discuss the situation with your buddies in a manner that demeans them or lowers others' impression of your associates. Don't forget that you were not born with the skills you currently possess. You had to learn and develop them. If that's true, it means there was a time when you were also ignorant and did not possess those skills. The fact that you developed the skills before your associates got the opportunity to do so does not make you better than them in

With gossip, we put into words, our low opinions of others.

any way. It simply puts you in a situation where you can invest in them by helping them develop the skills that they need to be successful.

Broken Promises

Remember Oliver? That's our friend from earlier who had a habit of arriving late for almost every meeting – until he spoke to Jill, one of his team members. Before the encounter with Jill, he always seemed to have a very good reason for each tardy moment:

> "My last meeting ran over time."

> "Someone stopped me on the way here."

> "I was busy doing something important and lost track of the time."

What Oliver did not realize initially was how this behavior was coming across to those waiting on him for those meetings to begin. Regardless of how good his reasons were for being late, many started recognizing it as a habit for him. It became a part of how people saw him. Tardiness was his identity. He became Oliver, the *Tardy*! This perception of him eventually started showing up in the non-verbal behaviors of his team members. Thankfully, he eventually got some clues from those.

Although he wasn't aware of it at the beginning, here's what his tardiness was communicating to those who worked with him:

> He doesn't care about my time.

> He doesn't respect me.

The Power of Respect

I can't rely on him.

He feels he's more important than the rest of us.

While he may not have meant to communicate any of these, that's how they saw his behavior. Several years ago, after checking into a hotel somewhere in the East Coast of the United States for a speaking engagement, I was waiting to get into an elevator when a group of people passed by. I heard one of them say, "I'm always late. It's the story of my life." Then, they started laughing about it.

Leaders who win the respect of others are the ones who deliver more than they promise, not the ones who promise more than they can deliver.

Mark A. Clement

Granted, these ladies were just speaking in a lighter mood, but to me, this is no laughing matter. And I don't think those waiting for that person each time she was late found it funny either. That type of attitude shows an absolute lack of respect for the people waiting for you. Keeping to time and not keeping others waiting is a sign of respect that says you value their time. It shows humility because you do not esteem your time as more important than theirs. One leader I worked with some years ago explained why she strives to always be on time at every meeting. She said, "Their time is valuable; my time is valuable."

But some don't see it that way. I know leaders who saw it as a badge of honor that people were waiting for them. This behavior fed their ego. They felt important that there were people waiting to see them. I've even seen situations where they kept people waiting longer for no apparent reason. They were not engaged in anything important at the moment people were waiting for them. They just kept people waiting, way past the time of appointment they had agreed to. Yes, there are times when circumstances can conspire to prevent us from keeping scheduled appointments. But that's not the situation here. This is an intentional time-wasting tactic designed to communicate their high view of their own importance to those waiting. For some, maybe they're just not aware of how that behavior comes across to those around them. No matter which reason it is, I think it's a good idea for you and me to rethink the issue. Here's how someone described to me how they feel about this:

> When I take time out of my schedule to meet with someone and they show up late with no apology or regrets, I feel disrespected, as if that person puts no value whatsoever on our time together.
>
> It makes me feel like if you don't value the time and effort, why should I? This is particularly egregious when this is the norm with that person and not the exception.[17]

Am I saying that if you arrive anywhere late, for any reason, then something is wrong with you? By no means! Even with the best of intentions, a perfect storm of conditions can come together to delay your on-time arrival on occasions. Where it turns into a problem is when this becomes a habit. When people can predict – with a high degree of accuracy – that you will be late, this is not a good sign. When you're always late, they begin to see you as unreliable. It speaks volumes about who you are. It starts to affect your integrity.

Here's what I know – if you plan to always be on time for everything, you will be on time most of the time. That's because the goal of arriving early will factor into when you leave your previous location, and what route you take to get to your next destination. If you plan to be on time, even those times when you arrive late will not catch you unawares. You would know before you arrived that you were going to be late, and because that goes against the core of who you are, it will bother you. Or does it even bother you at all? I hope it does! I think it should, because of what it communicates to those waiting on you.

"Upset and disrespected," is how Nair describes it. "When they show up late or don't show up at all, it's like they are saying that they don't respect me or my time."[7] For Kim, she finds it "disrespectful and selfish."[12]

Bob believes this is symptomatic of bigger issues, especially when it's a pattern. He said this makes him feel "disrespected or devalued. If I have committed my time to meet with you, I would hope that you would appreciate it enough to at least show up on time. Show me that you care; that this is important to you, too."[6]

I'm sure you can easily notice the pattern from these comments – disrespected and devalued is the theme. This is how most people feel as a result of the behaviors of those who take others and their time for granted. Is it your goal to make people around you feel disrespected or devalued? I hope that's not what you want. Instead, we want to make others feel valued and respected.

Now, for those few instances when you know you will be late, how do you handle them? People who are meticulous about keeping to time will realize, before the agreed time, that they won't make it to the scheduled meeting on time. What do they do? They make an effort to reach out ahead of time to inform the other party or parties of the situation, and let them know the reasons they won't make it on time. Because they take psychological ownership for anything they commit to, they also feel emotionally bound to follow through to completion. They know that their good name and reputation depends on it. They're not content with just explaining it away. They don't deal with it after the fact. They deal with it before. My good friend, Adekunle agrees. He said, "courtesy demands that you call and inform the other party of the new developments. I don't always feel good each time it happens because I believe in good time management."[18]

But what do you do if you have meetings stacked back-to-back and you find yourself running breathlessly to your next meeting? You can start by paying attention to how your meetings are scheduled. I know a leader who will not schedule three meetings in a row without a break or a *me-time* somewhere in-between to catch up, reflect on the meetings he has attended and have enough time to prepare for, and get to the next one.

If being late to a meeting seems of little consequence to you, you should know that others could and will infer your level of integrity from it; especially if that behavior becomes a pattern with you. They will see you as unreliable. Being on time for anything has an implied promise inherent in it. Your integrity as a person depends on fulfilling that promise. That's the reason that you cannot afford to be wishy-washy about delivering on promises, no matter how trivial or casual. It's also for this reason that you cannot afford to misuse other people's time.

The Time Taker

I was about to start elementary school when Motorola engineer, Martin Cooper invented the mobile phone in April 1973. As a result, it wasn't widespread then, as it is today. Even though landlines were available at the time, no one in my immediate family had one. Neither did anyone I was related to. At that time,

If you plan to always be on time for everything, you will be on time most of the time.

owning a telephone was the exclusive preserve of the rich and the educated in my part of the world. Most people did not have one in their homes. As a result, when you visited people, you just showed up at their front door.

I still remember how, while in high school, I would walk for almost two hours to my best friend's house just to hang out with him. And there were times when I would get there and he was not home, so I'd take another couple of hours to walk back home. This also happened to him a few times. Some days, as I walked to his house, I'd be praying quietly under my breath that even if he was not home, one of his siblings would be. That would enable me to at least, rest my feet for a while before embarking on the long walk back home. There were also a few times when our paths would intersect while I would be going to his house and he was heading to mine. In those instances, we would decide on whose house to go, based on which was closer or had food ready for us to eat!

If that were today, we'd probably just call (or text) each other to let the other person know we're on our way. But then, we had no phones, so nobody called to tell you they were coming for a visit. They just showed up unannounced at your door. For many of us today, especially in the western world, that's unthinkable. You dare not show up at someone's home without letting them know you're coming. Virtually everyone has a smart phone nowadays, so there's no excuse. But as I had just described, during my childhood, surprise visits were perfectly acceptable.

The Power of Respect

The amazing part is that usually, no one took offense to the presence of these unexpected guests. In fact, most people were largely delighted to see friends or family members that they've neither seen nor communicated with for months, or even years. (Except for in-laws you don't like, but that's a different story altogether!) Usually, the host family would go to great lengths to accommodate their guests and make them feel comfortable. Those were the good days!

Being on time for anything has an implied promise inherent in it.

Today however, people don't just show up at other's front doors unannounced. It's almost unimaginable. Most homes in the western world have front doors with either side panels or peep holes in them. If you hear the doorbell ring and you look through one of these to see an unfamiliar or unexpected face, you'd most likely not open the door to the unwanted intruder – unless you're new in the neighborhood, and they have come bearing gifts. Very few people will turn down a welcome gift from a family down the street. In general, most people today will call you on the phone to let you know they're coming. Some will even call you while standing outside your door to let you know they're there. These days, people won't usually just show up at your front door unexpected. But there's another way we do that exact same thing – show up unexpected and unannounced!

That's one thing I've come to realize about many of the phone calls that we make. Usually, they're not expected. Unless you have a prior arrangement to call someone on that day and at that time, they're likely not expecting your call, so that phone call is an intrusion into their lives at that moment, and a disruption of whatever it is they're currently engaged in. Has it ever occurred to you that your phone call is similar to just showing up at someone's door unannounced and uninvited? Yes, they have the choice of whether or not to answer the call, just like they have the choice of whether to open the door or not, but it's still an intrusion. When we call people out of the blue and immediately launch into the reasons for calling them, here are a few things that this behavior may be unintentionally communicating:

I don't care about what you're doing; I will disrupt it to have my way.

My time's more important than yours, so I can take a portion of your time anytime I want.

It's all about me, and I need your attention now!

I don't respect your time.

I know that this is not really what many of us are saying. Neither is any of this what we want to communicate when we call people without warning. But can you at least see the possibilities of how it could come across?

Am I saying that we shouldn't call people except in instances when they're expecting our call? Absolutely not! All I'm asking is that we respect their time. Time is one of the most important and valuable resources that any one of us have today. And because I know how valuable my time is to me, I can appreciate how valuable your time is to you as well.

So, what should we do when we call people who are not expecting such calls? I think simply asking for their permission is a good place to start. Over the last several years, I've learned that one of the first sentences out of my mouth when I make such calls should be,

"Do you have a moment to talk?"

"Is this a good time?"

"Can you talk now?"

By asking these questions, you're showing that you are respectful of their time and attention, and you're giving them the opportunity to decide whether or not they want to invest that time talking to you, instead of just taking it without their consent.

Consider how it makes you feel when you're busy working on something for which you need full concentration when a phone call you're not expecting comes in. You answer the call, and the person starts talking without checking to make sure it's a good time for you. Even if you know and love them, you may not really have the time to talk to them at that moment. Now, you're torn between either finding a nice way to tell them to get off the phone or just abruptly cutting off the line! If you stay on the call, you lose your focus from your task by the time you're done talking to them. This can be frustrating because it takes a significant amount of time to get back to the same level of concentration on the work you were doing before being rudely interrupted[19]. In other instances, a build-up of situations like this can lead to stress over time.[20] If not handled properly, it could blow up suddenly without notice.

Let's look at another scenario. Take the situation in which a friend or colleague walks into your office without notice and starts talking to you, interrupting whatever you may be doing at that time? How does it make you feel? Do you leave what you're doing and give them your attention? Or maybe you just continue doing what you were doing, while they blab away. By the way, ignoring them is not a good decision either, which is what some of us do with the hope that they will take the hint and leave. But imagine how you would feel if this were done to you. Remember that feeling and avoid doing the same thing to somebody else.

Ivan and Denys are two friends who migrated from their native country of Ukraine to settle in Canada. They also found themselves working with the same organization in the city of Edmonton. They did not arrive in Canada at the same time, neither did they know each other at all prior to finding themselves working in the same company. They also work

A sudden, unexpected phone call is an intrusion into someone's life – an intrusion that disrespects their time.

in different departments – Ivan is an engineer while Denys worked in finance. In addition, Ivan had been living in Edmonton for almost ten years before Denys' arrival. Since the time they first bumped into each other at the cafeteria, their common historical origins have brought them together.

Soon, Denys started dropping by Ivan's office unannounced to ask questions. At first, Ivan was happy to help his fellow countryman, who was new in the city. After a while, the visits became more frequent and the questions did not warrant the disruptions Ivan was experiencing each time his friend stopped by. Also, Denys did not seem to be in a hurry to leave each time he came for a visit. His conversations tended to be long and winding to the extent that Ivan started getting frustrated and irritated, mainly because of the disruptions to his work. He began to find polite ways of either telling or showing Denys that he was busy without offending him. But our friend was clueless.[21] How frustrated do you think this is leaving Ivan each time it happens? Now, put yourself in Denys' position. Do you behave this way without realizing the impact of your behavior on the other person? In order to not be the annoying person who doesn't have a clue when interrupting others, I've found a very good way to handle this: I send them a text or instant message.

Let me pause here to say that when it comes to communication, I don't particularly recommend the use of texting and similar forms of instant messaging as the primary medium of choice. Face-to-face should always be considered first. If that's impossible, then use the telephone. I think texting should be used as a last resort. However, if the goal is not to be intrusive, but a way to get them to agree to a phone call or an in-person discussion, it's perfectly okay to use instant messaging to gauge someone's readiness for a discussion. In these cases, I've learned to send text messages such as,

> "I need to talk to you. When's a good time for me to call?"

> "Do you have a moment to talk within the next hour?"

They don't have to read the message at the very moment it arrives. Neither do they have to respond right away. Yes, I know quite a few people who take pride in how quickly they can answer instant messages, but that's their choice. They can respond at their own time with a good timeframe for you to call them or have that in-person discussion. With this approach, you ensure that you're not just "taking" their time from them without their approval.

The Power of Respect

You're not behaving as if your time is more important than theirs. You're showing humility in the way you respect their time. Still, the way you see them is a very strong unconscious factor in how you value their time.

Seeing Others Clearly

Our social environment early in life could have a profound effect on whether or not we are humble. Most of the time, what we experience during our growing years go a long way in shaping our views and values. This reminds me of an incident that happened years ago.

It was the first day back at work after the Christmas holidays. I was standing in line at the cafeteria checkout, lunch in hands. When it was my turn to pay, I smiled at Nancy, the cashier, and said,

"Hey Nancy! How are you today?"

"I'm good. Thank you." She responded.

Probing further, I asked, "How was your holiday? Did you travel or stayed in town?"

Her face lit up with a smile as she told me that she had spent the holidays with her son. He's an engineer and had been in India for about a year on a three-year contract. She was happy that she could spend the holidays with him, his wife and their little boy. From the way she recounted how she spent the holiday season, I could tell that she must have had an unforgettable experience.

Moments later, as I settled down to eat with Frank, my colleague with whom I had gone to lunch, he asked,

"What's going on with you? I saw you talking excitedly to that cafeteria woman."

I responded that I was just asking if she had a good time away from work, and wanted to know how she spent her holidays. His next comments baffled me.

"Why?! You don't have to talk to her! She's just a cafeteria worker! She's beneath you!"

NOTHING HIGHER

To Frank, Nancy was just a nameless person who worked in the cafeteria. She was not a person that he needed to give the light of day. After lunch that day, I began to think of how many times I may have treated other people as if they don't matter. I wonder how many of us see others the way Frank saw Nancy – people to be seen, not heard; folks to put up with, instead of appreciated. Some of us treat people as objects to be used to achieve our selfish ends and purposes. The most deceptive part of this is that some of these behaviors are so subtle and unconscious that we don't even realize that we exhibit them.

Frank did not see anything wrong in his comments to me. Although we both live in the United States, he grew up, like me, in a different part of the world. He was raised in the type of culture where the elite do not typically mingle with the middle-class and low-class people. His parents were rich, and they had several helpers or servants in their huge and expansive estate.

The way you see people is the way you treat them. And, the way you treat them is the way they often become.

Benjamin Disraeli

These people just worked for them. Their value lay only in the services they provided. The entire family knew nothing about the personal lives of those who worked in their spacious mansion. At the time we sat at lunch together, Frank was a leader in the organization we were both working with. Even though he had lived in the United States for more than two decades, he had yet to learn how to relate to people appropriately; how to treat them with respect.

Unfortunately, today's western culture further diminishes the impact of respect. It's filled with music, books, television shows and movies that seem to elevate arrogant and disrespectful attitudes. We appear to celebrate behaviors that are borderline abusive towards other people. Some even see it as just harmless comedy. As a result, we are becoming numb to the effects that these actions have on meaningful relationships. But there's something to be said for treating others with courtesy and respect; for valuing them as people with hopes and dreams.

I know that many people are polite to others they consider

The Power of Respect

better than themselves; or to those who have something that they want. It may be a boss we want to curry favor with or someone with whom we want to do business. But to people that we see as beneath us socially, politically, or economically, some of us can become very disrespectful. We may think these people have no value to add to us. So, we treat them as if they're nothing. We neither recognize nor acknowledge them. As a result, we miss whatever value they could add to our lives.

In his blog, *The Importance of Respect in Teams,* Assad Schuitema explained why some of us have the tendency not to respect others. He wrote, "Some people think that showing respect is somehow degrading. They feel that the weak people show respect to the strong and powerful just because they are weak. This is a complete misunderstanding. It does not show weakness to

> *If you have some respect for people as they are, you can be more effective in helping them become better than they are.*
> John W. Gardner

see the value in others. It shows immense strength. It shows that someone is secure enough in their own value to be able to look out onto the world to see the value that is out there."[22]

When you don't respect people, you don't see the value in them. When you don't see their value, you won't recognize their natural talents. Once this happens, you miss out on the opportunities to help them leverage those talents into strengths. And you deny yourself of the positive value they could have added to your life. That's because the lack of respect can be seen in your behaviors towards them. You may not see it, but they do, and you end up losing their trust.

This is especially important for leaders. And when I say leaders, it's not limited to C-Suite executives and those who lead teams. I mean every one of us. You don't need a fancy title to be a leader. We are all leaders within our respective spheres of influence. In his book, *Leading Change,* James O'Toole proposes that "what creates trust, in the end, is the leader's manifest respect for the followers." When leaders do not respect those they influence, it is a symptom of more fundamental problems such as insufficient humility and too much ego. Whether you agree or not, disrespecting people you consider unimportant or uninfluential says a lot about your character.

In the blog post I referred to earlier, Mr. Schuitema commented on the benefits of respecting others. He said, "It is also important to remember that respect is reciprocal. When you respect someone, you will recognize the value in them. You will treat them in such a way that tells them you find them valuable. The natural response on their behalf is to respect you in return. They will feel that this person really does add value to my life. They magnify what is good about me. They bring out the best in me. When you do this for someone, they will view you as very valuable to them and they will develop a deep respect for you."

Have you heard of what is known as the Waiter Rule? It refers to a common belief that a person's true character can be gleaned from how they treat service workers, such as a waiter. In a 2006 *USA Today* article,[23] Del Jones described some interesting experiences a few CEOs had when they were younger. Many of them maintained that how you treat a waiter can predict a lot about your character. Part of the article also described how this could be tied to the way people were raised.

Several years ago, I was having lunch at a restaurant with a friend, who is also a pastor. As we settled down to place our orders, he asked our waitress for her name and asked if she had anything that she's concerned about, for which we could pray. She lit up immediately, and shared a few of her concerns with us. As my friend prayed over our meal that day, he also prayed for her. Even though she did not see us pray for her, the fact that my pastor friend asked her the question made her day. Of course, we also left her a good tip!

You can judge a person's character by the way he treats people who can neither help him nor hurt him.

Can you imagine what could happen if we all treat people who cross our paths in a similar manner? Or what the impact would be when leaders, in the true spirit of being servant leaders, extend some courtesy and respect to the people they lead? It's a game changer! And our world will start becoming a much better place.

What You Get

When you respect someone, it means you won't try to take advantage of them or abuse them. You see the value in them, so you care about them. Respect also begets respect. As you show humility by respecting others, you will earn a deeper respect from them in return. That's because "when we walk in humility, we're authentic, and people respect us because of our authenticity."[24]

There are so many opportunities that we get on a daily basis to treat people who cross our paths with serious consideration of their worth and value. When you and I behave in ways that show respect to others, the benefits are countless. Here are a few:

1. Instead of people getting frustrated, disappointed, furious and resentful toward you, their perceptions about you begin to change. They get feelings of positive emotions. With that, they want to work and collaborate with you. You're able to get things done faster and better, rather than being resisted everywhere you turn.

2. With those that may be considered beneath you, either because of what they do or their position, treating them with respect will attract a lot of goodwill to you from them. That's because your behavior towards them will be distinctly different from how others treat them. You never know how they could add value to you in the future.

3. Looking for opportunities to do something good for others and to help them demonstrates the value you place on them and their importance, rather than yours. Apart from the joy that you bring them, there are huge benefits for you also. The paybacks from altruism have been well documented with countless studies and research. You're happier, which in turn reduces your stress level. Some studies have linked this to longer life, improved physical well-being and mental

health.

4. If you lead a team of people at work, showing kindness and respect to your associates and giving them a second chance when they mess up is one way to show them how much you value them. Your gentle and compassionate response to their miscues can help build loyalty in them – loyalty to you as their leader and to your organization.

What You Can Do

Valuing other people and giving consideration for their time, abilities, and resources go a long way to show the level of respect that you have for them. This type of respect says, "I don't see my time, resources and abilities as more important than yours."

Here are a few things you can start doing to improve in this area:

1. Be brave and ask those closest to you for honest feedback on how they see your behaviors and the impact on them.

2. Schedule time regularly to volunteer to do the kind of work that you may have thought is beneath you. Talk to the people who do such work, with an attitude to learn from them. You'd be surprised by what you may learn.

3. Refrain from sharing negative or damaging information about others with those who are neither a part of the problem nor a part of the solution. Consider your true motivations before saying things that portray others negatively.

4. Consider what your implicit biases are. How do you subconsciously see people who are different from you? Begin making efforts to see everyone as a unique, valuable human being created in the image of the Creator.

When we respect others and see the value in them, we don't focus on our own importance. However, nothing speaks of self-importance more than the person who behaves as if they have all the answers. In the next chapter, we look at why the humble know-it-all is an oxymoron.

CHAPTER 6
DO YOU REALLY KNOW?

Knowledge is proud that it knows so much;
wisdom is humble that it knows no more.

- William Cowper

When it happened on April 20, 2010, it was the biggest such disaster in US history. Named the *Deepwater Horizon Oil Spill*, the explosion on the semi-submersible oil drilling rig in the Gulf of Mexico killed eleven people. By the time it was over, an estimated 4.9 million barrels of crude oil had been leaked. The result was an environmental disaster of huge proportions.

While the rig operator, Transocean and the contractor, Halliburton were also found to be at fault, most of the blame was laid squarely by investigators at the feet of oil giant, British Petroleum (BP). How the fallouts from this accidental tragedy were handled by BP leadership eventually became a much bigger news item than the disaster itself.

In an interview with the British Broadcasting Corporation (BBC) in May 2010, BP CEO, Tony Hayward tried to shift the blame by saying, "This was not our accident. This was not our drilling rig. This was Transocean's rig. Their systems. Their people. Their equipment."[1]

A few weeks later, a slightly more remorseful Mr. Hayward said, "A number of companies are involved, including BP, and it is simply too early – and not up to us – to say who is at fault."[2] In the weeks that followed, he continued to defend his company and made utterances that showed a complete lack of sensitivity to the plight of all the people and families affected by the disaster. At one time, during an attempt at being apologetic to those impacted, he said, "I'm sorry. We're sorry for the massive disruption it's caused their lives. There's no one who wants this thing over more than I do. I'd like my life back."[3]

That last sentence received a lot of backlash. Many thought he was so self-absorbed that even at the moment of contrition, his focus was still on himself and the effect the situation had on him – *I'd like my life back.* And he definitely tried to get his life back as news reports captured him engaged in a sailing race, where he was competing with his yacht. This happened while the mess created by the spill was still being cleaned up. By July 2010, BP's Board of Directors had had enough and announced that Tony Hayward would be replaced as CEO by October of the same year.

Personally, I don't think the oil spill disaster caused Mr. Hayward to lose his lucrative job. Other executives have survived worse situations. His awkward and insensitive responses to it were responsible for his dilemma. In a July 2010 CNN report, correspondent, Allan Chernoff implied that Tony Hayward's lack of humility and empathy appeared to have cost him his job. He said, "A nation furious at the environmental and economic catastrophe needed to see a contrite, compassionate CEO. Instead, BP sent what appeared to be a pompous foreigner."[4]

No one is immune from making mistakes, especially one that was precipitated by such an unexpected event as the Deepwater Horizon spill. However, people's core values and character tend to be revealed when they are under pressure. When trouble comes, what's inside tends to bubble to the surface and show up. For Tony Hayward, his values and how he saw himself showed up in the way he responded to this disaster.

Confronted with a number of scientific studies showing evidence that large clouds of oil were forming deep underwater

Do You Really Know?

where they could damage Gulf sea-life, he opted for denial instead, and was adamant in his arrogant assertion that there was no underwater spill beyond what was seen on the surface at that time. He said, "The oil is on the surface. There aren't any plumes."[5] He was a geologist after all, so he understood what was going on better than the average person. Or so he thought. He reportedly told *The Guardian* in an interview that the oil spill was "relatively tiny" compared to the "very big ocean."[6]

As intelligent as we are as humans, we don't know everything. In fact, not a single one of us *can* know everything. But our behaviors sometimes belie that fact. Some of us walk around as if we are the living embodiment of *Encyclopedia Britannica*. We think we know so much that our decisions and actions are infallible; that we don't make mistakes. People in leadership positions are more susceptible to this. As a leader, you may not think that you need to explain your decisions and how they are reached to your associates. In order to drive engagement, however, you do; especially when you've made a mistake. Jim Whitehurst, the author of the book *The Open Organization*, once wrote:

> Being a leader doesn't mean that you're always right or that you won't err. What being a leader does mean is airing the reasons for why you did something and then making yourself accountable for the results – even if those you're accountable to don't directly work for you.[7]

When leaders do not take responsibility for their mistakes, the result is an atmosphere of distrust within the team. While this is important for those who lead teams of people in the workplace, it is equally essential for every one of us. We need this in order to build trust with, and earn the respect of those with whom we associate. The truth remains that even when you think that you know, you want to have enough humility to hear others out and learn from them.

I'll confess that this was an area of struggle for me, especially on the home front. For example, I did not think I needed to explain my decisions to my children, especially when they were young. I grew up in an African culture where children were seen and not heard. If you made a mistake, you doubled down and expected them to just take it. They're your children, after all. You're the parent. How dare they question your judgment? That's the height of disrespect. Of course, I did not know any better at the time. But as they grew older, I began to see the need to shed my pompous tendencies. I realized the importance of explaining why I made some decisions and owning up to my mistakes. I later realized that it's not just me. Many of us naturally don't like owning up to our mistakes.

Why is it that we generally don't want to admit our mistakes? My theory is that it's because we don't like the way an admission makes us look. They make us look bad, and we hate the potential consequences. This seems to be in our nature. Remember when you were younger and wanted to play with the same toy that one of your siblings was playing with? You grabbed hold of the toy from one end, while your brother or sister was clutching the other end of it. Both of you began to pull it from side to side, and suddenly it got ripped apart. Immediately, each side dropped the broken piece in their hand, pointed to the other person and yelled, "He did it!"

In his book, *Your Brain at Work*, David Rock wrote that we behave in this manner because admitting to mistakes subconsciously lowers our perceived status. As a result, we feel less than other people. He wrote, "People don't like to be wrong because being wrong drops your status, in a way that feels dangerous and unnerving."[8] Human history has also taught us that depending on the level of depravity, we can go to extreme lengths to avoid or eliminate situations that can jeopardize and threaten our perceived important status. If care is not taken, we will do anything to sweep our mistakes under the rug so they never see the light of day.

One of the most common ways we tend to avoid this status drop is to instinctively compare ourselves with someone we see as worse. Other times, we use deflection by attacking the person who's trying to point out the mistake and tell them they do the same. Either of these responses validates Mr. Rock's view. The goal is to preserve the level of our perceived elevated status or importance and to make others look inferior when compared to us. This is because of our natural egotistic tendency. It happens because we have a high view of our own importance, and we don't want to let go of that high opinion. But this doesn't have to be the case. As you and I learn to be humble, we become more comfortable with owning up to our mistakes.

Learn of Me

Humble leaders not only own up to their mistakes, they also tend to use them as object lessons for others to learn from. A few years ago, I heard my pastor share a personal story during a Sunday morning sermon. In order to do justice to it, I'll recount it exactly as he shared it, in his own words:

> It was maybe twenty, twenty-five years ago, that we were having a women's breakfast at the church. The breakfast was in the lower level of the building, and that's also where the kitchen was. One of the other pastors and I got up early, real early, to go and cook the breakfast. Because we were there early, somehow inside of me, my heart was throbbing because I'm doing this great sacrifice for all the women.

> Men, I am something! Talking about sacrifice! I got up around 4:00 am. I really thought I was something! So, as the ladies would come by, I'd say, "Hi! Yep! I've been up since around 4 o'clock this morning for this."

> Somebody else would come by and I'd say, "I think I'm going to have to take a nap here pretty soon because you know …"

> Another person would come around, and I'd say, "I've been standing here since 4-something; I think my legs are gonna fall off."

> Finally, one of the deacons, in a very tactful, loving, and respectful way said, "Okay pastor, we get it. You got up early!"

I've been taking my bait out. He didn't just nibble
at my bait. He yanked it off the fishing pole,
threw it on the ground and stepped all over it right
there. And I got what I deserved.

Have you ever laid out a lure for people to affirm you in some
way? Have you ever used language, positioned yourself, said
things in a way, hoping maybe somebody will say something
positive or notice you, and afterwards you realize how insecure
you were? And why in the world did you need that in the first
place? How many of you know what it's like to bait other people
in order to get affirmation or praise?

Can you relate? Have you done something similar to this
before? Yeah! Many of us are guilty of this at some level. Now, I
have to pause here and say that this man, who recounted his
experience, is one of the humblest people I know. You only need
to spend a few moments with him to discover and appreciate his
level of humility and integrity.

But there he was, teaching about humility, and using his own
immodest example to prove the point. To be honest, I initially
found it difficult to believe that
what he had described actually
happened. My first thought was
that he made it up to illustrate a
point because the man I know
him to be is the complete
opposite of what he described.

*We will do anything to
sweep our mistakes
under the rug so they
never see the light of day.*

But a few weeks later, I asked him privately if the story was true,
and he confirmed that it was. Still, it's tough for me to
comprehend. That's because as I had said before – to me, he's
humility personified. After knowing him fairly well for several
years, I just couldn't imagine him doing what he described. Even
though it happened decades before I knew him, I still found it
difficult to believe. But this is what humble people do. They
readily admit their mistakes, and even use them to make a point!

Rarely would many of us make ourselves the butt of our own
jokes. Or point out where and when we have missed the mark. I
think it takes a humble heart to do that. And that's exactly what

great leaders do. They not only learn from their own mistakes but they also use them as examples so others can learn as well. If that were me, I'd probably put an imaginary person into that story so I wouldn't look foolish to others!

When leaders showcase their own struggles during their journey of personal growth – especially to those they lead – it does two things. First, they're giving legitimacy to the personal struggles, growth and learning of others. They are validating the normalcy of their team members' journeys of development. It's another way of communicating to their associates that they can work through these issues and overcome them, just as the leader has. One reason this becomes very important is that many of us subconsciously attribute superhero status to people we look up to – leaders, celebrities, sports stars or anyone in an important and visible role. By talking about their own struggles, they're saying, "I'm just like you. There's nothing special about me."

Second, by admitting their own mistakes and imperfections, they make it okay for others to be imperfect, too. We connect better with individuals who share their failures and flaws with us. In doing so, they appear more human. They look more like us. In fact, I've come to learn that this helps us withhold criticism about them in areas that we would have otherwise been very critical. When someone always appears to us as if they have everything together, we tend to find something to nitpick about. We rarely find complaints when they openly talk about their own imperfections. Ironically, those around them already know about those deficiencies anyway. People are simply waiting for them to admit what everyone can see.

We connect better with individuals who share with us, their failures and flaws.

Admitting the Obvious
As a speaker and business coach whose primary audience and client base is in North America, people sometimes come to me immediately after I've delivered a keynote at a conference and express surprise that I speak the English language very well. It seems many of these people did not expect me to speak good

English because I speak in an accent that is less familiar to most Americans. They thought I learned the language as an adult. I would then explain to them that I've spoken the English language virtually all my life – that I grew up in Nigeria, where English is the official language. I would also explain that my accent stems from two facts – I speak another local Nigerian language and while in Nigeria, I spoke the British brand of English.

In other situations when people attend a seminar or workshop that I facilitate, the responses are slightly different. In that setting, people typically complete an evaluation form. Over the years, I have received valuable feedback from these evaluations that has made me a better speaker. Some of the comments on the forms have also given me clues into how we sometimes unconsciously elevate some people just because they have a stage and we're in the audience. Conversely, few of the participants would see the evaluation form as an opportunity to vent their frustration in the kind of feedback they provide. While this is rare in my seminars, I've seen a few scathing remarks on those forms. Here's a couple of actual comments I've received in the past:

> "His accent is so thick; I couldn't understand one word he said."

> "You would think someone who's supposed to communicate would know how to speak well!"

What I found remarkable is that from the same group of people, I would receive several glowing comments about how I spoke clearly and without ambiguity. Interestingly enough, I never get those scathing comments when I speak in Europe or other parts of the world. Not even once! It only happens in the United States. Even then, these comments usually come from less than two percent of those in attendance. Despite that small number, this was a source of discouragement to me when I first started speaking. I used to be greatly affected by these remarks. Instead of paying attention to the majority of people who said positive things, my focus would be on the one or two with negative comments. Later, a personal coach suggested that I address it upfront whenever I'm in a seminar. And I did.

Do You Really Know?

My approach was to bring up my accent in a light-hearted manner during the first few minutes of the seminar or workshop. And the difference has been remarkable. The result was a complete wipeout of the scathing comments and complaints, even though they were very small to begin with. I've even had some come to me at the end to let me know that they understood me perfectly, that they had no problems with the accent. Of course, once in a while, there would be someone who complained, but even the viciousness of the criticism became somewhat muted. Since I started doing this, I've seen that the two percent complaint rate has shrunk to almost nothing. Most of the time, not a single person complains. In fact, I've had some attendees come to me and say things like, "I love your accent" or enter comments such as "His accent made the seminar more interesting" on the feedback form. I found it interesting that talking about my accent upfront eliminated the complaints, even though they were small to begin with.

Note that my accent is not a mistake. It is who I am; it's how I speak. But to some North American ears, it's an imperfection perceived by a few of those in my audiences. By acknowledging it and talking about it, I was able to connect better with those who hear me speak. Either way, acknowledging mistakes – whether real or perceived – helps us to connect better with others. When we do it, we communicate a lower perceived importance of ourselves to those around us. People see that and receive it as a symbol of humility which endears us to them. It helps us connect better with them.

Even though admitting the obvious can help build our influence with others, some do not understand that fact. They make mistakes but won't own up to them – even when it's glaringly obvious to everyone around them. From my experience in the corporate world, you often see this with some people who have a solid education but not the necessary experience for the job they've been given. When they make mistakes, they try to sweep them under the rug or find someone else to blame. It's never their fault. That was Maya's approach.

Not My Fault

Maya had two college degrees, but very little experience in leading teams. When she was first hired to lead, she came on very strong. She wanted everyone to know that she was in charge. She did not listen to experienced members of her team and seemed to want to control everything instead of partnering with a team that many in the organization knew to be very productive and loyal. After a few months on the job, the honeymoon was over. The disdain for her from the team was palpable.

One afternoon after a day of horrible winter weather, the team sat around a table for a monthly staff meeting. Maya was clueless about the heavy cloud of low morale and exhaustion her team was under. She went through a presentation, reading from her slides without as much as a glance at any of the others around the table. It was obvious to everyone there that she was just going through the motions because this was on her to-do list. At the end of her presentation, one team member had had enough and spoke up. The person asked if Maya was aware of the low morale, and what she planned to do to help the team focus on their primary mission. She looked stunned by the question, and after a very long and awkward silence, returned back to referencing and reviewing slides from her just-concluded presentation. She didn't (or maybe couldn't) respond to the question asked. Melanie, another member of the team, felt like saying something but decided against it because nothing positive would have come out of it.

After the meeting, Melanie asked to speak with Maya privately. Melanie asked her about the staff meeting and shared with her what she thought about others' feelings at the meeting. Maya seemed surprised by the feedback, but thanked Melanie for coming to speak with her.

At the next monthly meeting, Maya asked members of the team to briefly share any concerns they may have before she started with the day's business agenda. Melanie thought an apology to the team would have been appropriate, but none came. She felt that Maya had missed a wonderful opportunity to gain the team's loyalty and trust, but it seemed pride kept her from doing so. Soon, Melanie left the team.[9]

Do You Really Know?

It takes humility to own up to faults. When pride rules, it's difficult to admit a mistake. Even when the appropriate corrective action of admitting and apologizing for the mistake is obvious to all those involved, arrogant people don't seem to see it. They dig in their heels and maintain the false charade because they're always right. Since they refuse to see the errors of their ways, they may go to ridiculous extents to protect themselves. They could call you names and label you a liar.[10] They could lose the respect of those around them, but they don't seem to care.[11] They could throw others under the bus to cover up their mistakes,[12] but that doesn't matter to them. What seems most important to them is the protection of their ego at all costs. They want to maintain the appearance of being in full control. But those around them can easily see through the thin veil and recognize them for what they truly are – weak, ineffective and untrustworthy.

Do you behave like Maya? If you do, I think an immediate turn-around is in order. Apologize to your team, and let them know you did not know any better. Promise to turn over a new leaf, and follow through on that promise. As you show consistency with your new behaviors, morale will begin to improve within your team. What you saw as a weakness is actually a sign of strength that elevates your stock with those you're leading. You're only human after all.

To Err is Human

One day during his final year of high school, Scott was walking along one of the aisles in the classroom when he passed by a female classmate with her back turned towards him. The girl was in the process of taking a seat. Without thinking, Scott quickly pulled away the chair and continued walking as if he'd done nothing. The poor girl fell to the floor awkwardly, injuring herself. She looked around, saw no one nearby and concluded that she had just missed the chair. Nobody else had seen what happened, so Scott felt good that he had pulled a fast one on his classmate. That feeling did not last long. On seeing the injury that the girl sustained, he felt very bad for what he had done. But he said nothing! Scott got home that day and couldn't sleep. After three days of being riddled with guilt, he finally decided to confess his sins. He couldn't face his classmate, so he wrote her a letter and asked for her forgiveness.[13]

Have you ever done something that you regret? I'm sure you have! So, have I. We all make mistakes. It's one of our built-in functions as humans. There's not a single person that is perfect. The problem is not in the fact that we make mistakes; the issue is how we respond to the fallout from our mistakes. From ancient times, we've always had the tendency to favor self-preservation. We seldom own up to our blunders. Our first inclination is to cover them up, just like Scott did. It started in the Garden of Eden when Cain killed his brother, buried him and went about as if nothing happened.

For many of us, our conscience eventually catches up. It threatens to expose us for the fraud that we are. Some of us respond by fessing up to our crimes. A few of us confess because our mistake has been exposed to light, thus forcing us to be humble. Others own up because they feel remorse for what they've done. But there are also those who will turn a deaf ear in an attempt to silence conscience's voice of reason.

Some may say that what Scott did was just a harmless prank. Yes, someone got injured, but it was not life-threatening. The victim fully recovered, so he did not have to apologize, they may argue. But I believe what's really important is how he responded to the prompt from his conscience. He probably learned not to repeat that prank in the future. Also, it will help him develop the humility to own up to future mistakes quickly before they become too big to handle.

Imagine Scott as an adult twenty years later, who has just made a mistake at work. His first instinct may be to hide it or cover it up. But he's probably learned from experience that that's not a good idea. Such mistakes will almost always be discovered. Covering it up would most likely hurt him and his career more than owning up to the mistake itself. He could destroy trust in the process. Do you remember Watergate? The cover-up was much worse than the crime itself.

The ugly truth is that each one of us has a dark side. We must acknowledge and recognize this tendency in us – the inclination to want to do the wrong thing at times. Realizing that we're not

Do You Really Know?

beyond infallibility should humble us. It also helps us. When we quickly own up to our mistakes, and take active steps to avoid repeating them, we build trust with others. People are usually forgiving, no matter the magnitude of the mistakes, but we must show humility and own up to the mistakes right away. This also applies to what we don't know.

You Don't Know All

No one person knows everything, right? Not even Watson, the IBM cognitive technology computer that in the year 2011, was the hands-down winner on the TV show, *Jeopardy!* Actually, Watson doesn't even qualify to be in the discussion since it's not a person.

I don't think many people will dispute the fact that no one person on the planet knows everything. If that's the case, why then do we sometimes behave as if we do? In the heat of the moment, our natural disposition seems to be to defend the indefensible and act as if we know it all.

Let's listen in on this dialogue that took place at a family dinner table.

> **Mom** (to son): What was that you were watching just before coming to dinner?
>
> **Son**: "Ruthless Violations."
>
> **Mom**: Isn't that a bad TV show? Why are you watching it?
>
> **Son**: I don't think it's bad. Have you seen it?
>
> **Mom**: No, I haven't. But I'm sure it's bad. With a name like "Ruthless Violations," how good can it be?
>
> **Son**: It's not really that bad. It was a show originally created by the XYZ Network. Their shows are usually good.
>
> **Mom**: No, it's not from XYZ! It's a bad show!
>
> **Dad** (chimes in): Are you sure it's not from XYZ? You've not even checked it yet. And you

139

haven't seen the show.

Mom: Yes, I checked it! I know it's not from XYZ.

Dad: How do you know that it's not from XYZ?

Mom: I checked it last week!

Dad (with sarcasm): Really?! So, you knew that this discussion, about this particular show was going to come up, and you checked it then and could still accurately remember that it's not from XYZ? A show you haven't seen?

Mom: Yes, I remember!

Dad: Are you sure about that? So, there's not even a remote possibility that you could be confusing it with another show?

Mom: No, I'm not wrong! I'm very sure of it!

Finally, Dad kept quiet and said nothing more. Later that day, he checked and found that truly, the show was created by the XYZ television network. But he said nothing to his wife. He knew her. Saying something would only lead to more arguments, and he did not want any more of that.

This dinner table exchange shows the futility of trying to reason with people who behave as if they know everything. Ask them if they think they know everything when they're thinking rationally, and they'll probably tell you that they don't. However, their behaviors when they feel the need to be right would always contradict that admission. In that moment, they don't know that they don't know it all. If you behave like the mom in this dinner exchange, allow me a few moments to speak to you directly.

The place where this attitude is prevalent is a very dangerous place to be. It's a dangerous place to be because it's a place where learning and growth are stifled. Since you think you're right, you probably won't take the time to check out the facts after the argument is over. To you, it's done with. You've won. And that's what really matters to you, isn't it? You have to win at that very moment. As a result, you don't learn. You remain in your ignorant state on that subject. Someone who wants to learn and grow from the experience may try to check the facts once the argument is over. A reasonable person with some humility may even return to apologize if the facts turn out to be contrary to what they thought. But that's not you. Even in the rare cases when you do apologize, you have a tendency not to learn from your own mistakes. That's because the next time there's another opportunity to showcase your know-it-all tendency, you embrace it with gusto; you do not learn from your prior experiences. You don't need to learn. You know everything!

Except that you don't really know everything. But that doesn't stop you from offering unsolicited advice, dominating every conversation, becoming confrontational in meetings or trying to boss everyone around. You use words like *certainly*, *undoubtedly*, *definitely* and *undeniably* despite not having the facts to back them up. Daniel J. Boorstin said that "the greatest obstacle to discovery is not ignorance – it is the illusion of knowledge." You may think you know, but you don't. The illusion of knowledge is not knowledge; it's just an illusion. You have opinions about everything and you're quick to let everyone around you know what they are.[14] When you argue in favor of a point without entertaining the fact that you may be wrong, it's a little disturbing. What you're saying is that you know all there is to know about that situation or subject. This is highly improbable, even if you are an expert on the subject.

> *The greatest obstacle to discovery is not ignorance – it is the illusion of knowledge.*
>
> Daniel J. Boorstin

While attending a seminar some time ago, I heard the instructor say that our ego is usually tied to one of two things:

> I want to be right.

> I don't want to be wrong.

Then she asked each one of us in attendance to think and reflect on which of these two feeds our ego. She also gave us a third option – *I don't know.* At that moment, my immediate instinctive reaction was to reject the premise that I had an ego to begin with. So, in response to the activity, I chose the "I don't know" option. However, for no apparent reason, I became preoccupied with trying to resolve this in my mind for the remainder of the seminar.

The more thought of it, the clearer it became to me that there's really no sitting on the fence here. Subconsciously in our behaviors, most of us have a need either to be right or not be wrong. As I look at my own life, my approach to making decisions and my manner of engaging others in discussions, I discovered that mine is the need to not be wrong.

When you don't want to be wrong, you may end up with analysis paralysis. The risk of making the wrong decision becomes huge and staggering. You don't pull the trigger and do something because of the fear of making the wrong decision. This need to not be wrong also shows up when you disagree with others. You're quick to see the holes in others' arguments and you wonder why they remain so rigid about their assertion when it's so crystal clear (to you) that they're wrong. You don't claim to be right, but you *know* they're wrong. If this becomes a pattern with a particular individual, you may begin to resent them for it. In so doing, you devalue them and could begin to have a high view of your own importance.

If, on the other hand, you have a need to be right, your tendency could be to argue irrationally and stick to your guns even when everyone around you knows you're just making things up. But you don't care, as long as people give in to your claim that you're right. You argue blindly and make up the facts as you go. Yes, you make up the "facts" since you cannot be wrong and you have to find other ways to prove that you're right. What ends up happening is that you contradict yourself. But that doesn't dissuade you either. If they point out your contradictions, you simply tell them they heard wrong. The problem is not with what you said, it's in their hearing – they must have hearing problems. And it doesn't matter to you if everyone around seems to have heard the same thing. All of them are wrong, and you are right.

What's more ridiculous is that often, you don't argue just only on topics in which you consider yourself an expert. You do it even when you know that the other person – the one you're arguing with – probably knows more than you do, about that topic. But that is irrelevant to you in that moment. All you want to do is win the argument. In the process of arguing, you fail to learn from the person who knows better than you, and you're blind as to how your behavior comes across. It looks to others as if winning the argument is your fixated and singular goal. You may even agree that you enjoy arguing just to argue with others.[15] But those with whom you argue do not enjoy it, and they probably see your behavior as immature. You have to be right, even when you're wrong. And it doesn't matter that you claim to know what you may not. You will take the little that you know about the subject and argue it to its illogical conclusions.

As you argue irrationally, others begin to realize that no amount of reasoning or rational thought will work with you. Some may see your behavior as that of someone who wants to be noticed and likes to attract attention.[16] Others will see it as being rooted in insecurity and your quest for control and significance.[14] One major consequence of this is that no one will want to talk to you about anything of importance. They will avoid all or most conversations with you. That's because you frustrate them[17] and they know all they will get from you is more arguments that are based on nothing more than your unfounded opinions and raw, uncontrolled emotions. They avoid you for the sake of maintaining their own sanity.[14] In fact, when they unknowingly say anything that triggers this behavior from you, they recognize the symptoms from your initial response and quickly throw in the towel. They stay quiet because they don't want to fuel your argumentative fire.[18] They let you win, even if they have facts that dispute your point. They just won't go there with you. They avoid any interactions with you unless they need to. And you end up being the loser. You lose the respect of those in your sphere of influence – your community.[19] You lose because you won't learn or grow from the exchange of ideas that could have happened if you were not known for this behavior.

When this is your approach, you don't learn. You can't learn. You continue to live in your ignorance simply because you don't want to admit to being wrong. You have a need to be right, so you come across as someone who believes they know everything.

Lazlo Bock, former senior vice president of People Operations at Google said, "Without humility, you are unable to learn." It takes humility for us to set aside what we think we know in order to consider another person's opinion. As we do this, learning and growth happens. Without it, we can become stagnant and stale in what we think we know.

It would be helpful for you to step back, take a deep breath, and decide if this hill of always being right, is one on which you're willing to die. You can ask yourself a few questions:

> Could there have been new developments that I'm not aware of?
>
> Do I really know all there is, about this situation?
>
> Why is it so important for me to be right or win this argument?
>
> Can I really be right, and everyone else wrong?

These reflective questions can help anyone begin the journey into seeing how their ego could be blinding them from seeing how they come across to others.

In March 2017, I was delivering a series of one-day seminars on emotional intelligence across five cities in the US states of Ohio and West Virginia. The last day was in Beckley, WV. Unlike all the other days, this one had an unusually low number of people in attendance. With only fourteen participants, I was able to see everyone very clearly throughout

Without humility, you are unable to learn.
Lazlo Bock

the day. One of them was a guy that was sitting on the back row to my right. From the beginning, his body language told me he did not want to be there. It's possible that somebody (maybe his boss) signed him up for the seminar and told him to attend. Throughout the day, he refused to respond to questions or contribute during group discussions; neither did he participate in any of the class exercises. Later that day, after the seminar was over, I went through the evaluation forms completed by the participants. It was very easy for me to spot which one was his – he was the only one who did not include his name. Here's what he wrote in the comments section:

> "An engineer has no business teaching emotional intelligence."

He knew that I have an engineering background because I usually share that information at the very beginning of this particular seminar. For most of the one-day event, I use stories of my personal and professional experiences to drive home the salient points of the seminar, highlighting my initial struggles and subsequent growth in the area of emotional intelligence, and how this later led me to pursue certification as an emotional intelligence coach and speaker.

But it seemed our friend never got past that first half-hour of the day when I told them about my initial training as an engineer. In his mind, I had no business speaking about, or facilitating a seminar on emotional intelligence. Even though he was physically sitting there the rest of the day, he had already checked out emotionally within the first few minutes. He was not ready to learn.[20] So he got nothing from that day's seminar. As a result, he had literally wasted a whole day of his life.

This is what happens when someone does not have enough humility to learn from people they come across. When you see someone, and you immediately think they have nothing to offer you, either because of where you met them, how they speak, what they look like, who they are or whatever other prejudiced impressions you may come up with, you are the one who loses at the end of the day. You are the one who has missed out on an opportunity that could have been of value to you. As H. Jackson Brown Jr. puts it, "Every person that you meet knows something you don't; learn from them."

Humility is far away from the know-it-all. So is the opportunity to learn and grow. Dr. Pamela Paresky, a psychologist wrote that "beginning at a position of intellectual humility was the only method of seeking truth, with no guarantee of finding it."[21] In other words, Dr. Paresky is saying that seeking knowledge and finding truth is only possible when we approach such endeavor with humility.

Why don't you resolve, starting today, to hear the other person out and consider their point of view, no matter how ridiculous it may seem to you at first? Admit that you don't know everything. Even if you do know a lot about the subject, you may still learn something. Socrates, the great philosopher, was reputed to have said, "True knowledge exists in knowing that you know nothing."

Resist the temptation to argue about what you don't know. You already know that you have that tendency. Think daily about what you will do differently. If necessary, schedule time on your calendar several times a day for reminders to resist the urge. This may be helpful when those reminders are just before meetings or interactions that usually induce this behavior. Finally, you can ask others to hold you accountable. Allow those who have seen this behavior in you to help you make the change you desire. Asking for others' opinions may be a good place to start. You will begin to see improvements as you take these to heart and act on them.

Every person that you meet knows something you don't; learn from them.

H. Jackson Brown Jr.

A Penny for Your Thought

Similar to the know-it-alls are those who enjoy debating everything in sight. To them, every topic is a chance to showcase the salient points of what they know. For these people, arguments are the order of the day. They delight in the opportunity. Their focus is on convincing others and winning arguments. As a result, they become obsessed with proving the validity of their own points even when it makes no sense to do so. In the process, they miss out on the opportunity to learn from others.

For some of these people, their arguments can become so blinding and the need to win so strong, that even when facts contrary to their opinions are presented to them, they don't see it. Or maybe they just choose not to see it. They can resort to falsehood and coercion in order to win. If they are in a leadership position, they may pull rank on you. They have no problem telling you that they know better.

If you're a leader given to this kind of behavior, what do you think this communicates to your associates? For how long do you think they will endure such acts from you? The honest truth is that they will eventually become tired of arguing with you. Rather than engage you in a debate, they may just let you be, in order to keep the peace, even when they know you're wrong. After all, you're the boss. You call the shots. But it will be your loss. You lose the trust and respect of your people, and you won't learn from others.

A good leader is humble enough, not only to entertain different points of view, but to also actively seek them out. I used to work for a leader who would not leave a meeting until everyone had contributed to the discussion. He wanted to know if there were any dissenting views or opinions, as well as the reasonings behind them. He would go around the room, call each person by name, and ask for their thoughts concerning the issue being discussed. On a few occasions, someone's gut-feeling, backed with cogent reasons, have resulted in a changed direction on an issue that everyone thought was previously settled.

Still, there are other times when the leader's opinion remains the best approach even after considering all others. Despite this, a great leader may consider going with another's idea just for the purpose of "conceding defeat," especially if that idea does not prevent the team from achieving its stated objectives. Yes, a humble leader will sometimes park their ideas for that of a team member. By doing so, they communicate to their team members that their opinions are valued and that their contributions are welcomed, even when they differ from the leader's.

True knowledge exists in knowing that you know nothing.
Socrates

Most leaders have stated goals that they want to see accomplished by the teams. But inclusive leaders are humble enough to suspend their own agendas and beliefs, no matter how strong. They will listen to, and consider the opinions of others. In so doing, they not only increase their own wealth of knowledge, but also validate the unique perspectives of their team members. More importantly, they earn the respect and trust of those team members.

Leaders who behave this way are forward-looking. They realize that teamwork is what makes the dream work, so they ensure that the ideas and opinions of their team members are heard. Personally, I think this also relieves the leader of the unnecessary pressure that sometimes comes with the unfounded expectation that they must have all the answers or come up with all the ideas needed to solve every problem. Yes, the final decision is theirs, but they don't have to do all the heavy lifting to arrive at that decision. Great leaders intentionally do this to develop their people and get them ready for the next level.[22]

I once worked for a manager who feared losing his job to those of us on his team. To guard against this fear, he made himself indispensable and put little or no efforts into developing members of the team. This is a very short-sighted behavior. If you develop your team members to the level where that they can take over your job, I think that frees you to move up to the next level in your career. This also gives members of your team a sense of belonging[23] and lets them know how invested you are, in their career development and growth. A very good understanding and deep cooperation within the team is the result. Team members would have the feeling that they have your backing, trust and support.[24] The result is that you also secure their trust and support.

Uncertainly Ambiguous
In today's business environment, ambiguity and uncertainty are commonplace. There are a lot of gray areas everywhere, especially when it comes to formulation of ideas and making decisions. But some of us act as if we have all the answers. If you're known to exhibit this behavior, there are times when it may just make a fool out of you. That's what happened to Janet.[25]

Janet was a production manager at one of the plants for a large multinational manufacturer and marketer of branded consumer foods that are sold through retail stores. To her, she was always right, and she did not realize how this had formed perceptions

Do You Really Know?

about her among the production staff. One day, as she was speaking to somebody on the production floor, she overhead a conversation about someone being pregnant. Instead of trying to find out who it was, she thought she knew. But she was wrong. Hours later, she approached one of the operators and

A humble leader will sometimes park his ideas for that of the team member.

congratulated her on her pregnancy. This turned into an awkward exchange as she walked away, and the person she congratulated looked confused. But no one corrected her. Before long, the rumor had spread

around about her being wrong in congratulating someone about a pregnancy. It eventually got back to her several days later, and she was embarrassed. Those in her department found it funny, but not Janet. She wasn't trusted within her own team because she always assumed that she was right. She was a know-it-all. After a few months, she quit her job and left for another company because the animosity towards her from the team was too great. She only lasted one year in the position.

Congratulating the wrong person was trivial and most people would laugh about it with others, but it was different for Janet. Because of her pattern of behavior that had showcased a know-it-all and condescending attitude over time, she was not trusted within her own team. As a result, the environment became toxic because of her, and she had to look for another job.

In some cases, those with this behavior may not even realize that they are advocating ideas as if they have all the answers. When you use words such as "certainly" or "undoubtedly" in situations where there are no facts to back up your claims, you're communicating the fact that your assertions are absolutes. This is the perception whether you realize it or not. In communicating opinions, thoughts or ideas, it's important to be clear that they're just that – your opinions. And these are opinions that could be flawed or not grounded because you may not have all the facts or the evidence to back them up. It's good to be tentative in those views so others can be invited to scrutinize them. Failure to do this can be a magnet for strong opposition. That may not be your intention, but this outcome is a possibility. You may be defeating your own purpose as a result.

Even in cases when you're sure of the facts, and you have the evidence to back up your claims, that doesn't mean that you know all there is to know about the subject. Someone who is humble realizes that no matter how much they know, they could learn more. They realize that there could be room for improvement. When leaders admit that they may not have all the answers, opportunities are created for others to come forward and offer solutions. Consider the case of John, who is the leader of a team of information technology professionals.

Each week during the team's recurring meetings, questions that required an explanation or answer about certain job situations were thrown at him. In a few cases, John would admit that he did not have an immediate answer. He would then ask his team members who have ideas about the issue to share those with the rest of the team. As a result of this well-known behavior, his team members viewed him as someone who is open and who respects the ideas of others.[26]

For the last few years, I have learned to adopt this approach when a participant asks me a question during a seminar or workshop. Even when I have what I think is the right response to the question, I first ask others in attendance if they have anything to say or contribute as a response. Here's what I found out: after others have chimed in with their own thoughts, the overall response is much richer and fuller than if I alone had responded. We end up with deeper insights than would have otherwise come from my response alone. In some cases, I *Someone who is humble realizes that no matter how much they know, they could learn more.* have learned from the collective wisdom shared, either directly or indirectly. Sometimes, one word or a phrase from another person triggers a thought that I had never considered before then. After experiencing the enrichment that I have enjoyed many times over through this approach, I always look forward to people asking questions just for the purpose of allowing others to contribute so we can all have a much more fulfilling experience.

Do You Really Know?

When leaders admit that they don't have all the answers, there's a sense of interdependence. Other team members soon realize that the best solutions come when there's reliance on one another to work through complex and vague problems. Also, the leader is respected by the team,[27] and this helps to build trust within the team. They see their leader as confident and selfless[28] – someone who is not only concerned about themselves and their reputation, but willing to put the needs and success of the team above all else.

Empowering others to lead, is a mark of a truly inclusive and humble leader. When leaders take the back seat and allow roles to be reversed, they model a situation where different perspectives are permitted to come into the fray. This is especially important when working in culturally diverse teams.

The Follower Leader
Many years ago, I was in a leadership gathering. During the meeting, the person who was the head of the team said nothing. If you did not know who he was, you would not have guessed that he was the boss, that the buck stopped with him. He wasn't running the meeting, so he didn't say much. He simply asked some clarifying questions and made a few comments. He did not challenge anyone's assertions nor did he force his ideas on the team. He just listened.

While there's great value in having the leader take charge sometimes, being a leader doesn't mean you have to run the show at all times. Unfortunately, in more than two decades of working in large corporate environments, I encountered people who believe that you don't have leadership abilities or potential if you don't always visibly show what they consider "leadership behaviors." To these people, you have to say something at every meeting. They believe that you must always have something to contribute, or you don't belong in leadership circles. These people expect every leader to exhibit a Type A personality, even if that's not who they are.

From my experience, people in the technical professions are more likely to be guilty of this. As an engineer, I saw many instances of this scenario in the course of my career. People "contributed" in meetings, not because they had something to say, but so that they would be seen as having said something. I have been in meetings where we seemed to go around in circles echoing the same things over and over. At the end of the day, nothing concrete was accomplished.

Personally, I have discovered that one of the most powerful and effective leadership traits is the deliberate choice of insignificance. This also happens to be a strong quality of humility. There's a pervasive and compelling aura of dignity that saturates the environment when someone who's the leader decides to take a back seat occasionally. They do this so that some other person can take the lead and shine. Choosing to appear insignificant or electing not to be noticed in spite of who you are is a sign of humility. Such leaders go out of their way to *not* be noticed, and to *not* receive affirmation. That's because true humility tends to prefer insignificance over self-promotion.

I have also discovered the great value in the leader asking questions instead of making assertions. I'm not talking about a situation where the leader has no answer. I'm speaking of instances where she believes that she knows the right course of action. But instead of communicating her decision, the leader instead engages the team, asking them questions to come up with a solution to a situation for which the leader believes she already has a solution. Why would she do this? Won't that be a waste of time? She already has a solution; why not just give it to them, and lay out her well-thought-out plan?

You do this because you may have thought through the plan, but your team hasn't. If you just tell them what they need to do to execute your well-thought-out plan, you may get compliance, but not the passion to make the execution successful. It could turn out to be another case of, "Well, that's what the boss wants us to do!" And explaining your thought process to them may not be enough. What's more important is that the team experiences the thought process just like you have. Going through the process with them will help you secure the necessary buy-in from the team, especially if it's essential to a successful execution.

So, even though the leader already has a solution, she chooses humility and goes to the team with the problem. She then facilitates the discussion that leads to a team solution. In many cases, new insights that the leader did not think of emerge, simply because of the collective wisdom of the team. Since they're part of the process, team members feel their contributions have been sought out and valued. They own both the process and the solution, so they're more invested in it. What comes with that is the passion to execute the decision and make it a successful outcome. This is unlikely to happen if the leader just announces the problem, and then gives the team the solution she has already come up with.

If you lead a team or an organization, it doesn't mean that you know everything or have all of the answers. Your position doesn't require you to come up with all the ideas on your own. You may even be a subject matter expert in an area, but you still shouldn't assume you know it all, and therefore make decisions to dictate or lord things over those you lead. Your subject matter expertise doesn't include leadership. No one knows everything. Your job is to explore and ask questions that will lead your people to the same conclusions that you may have reached. That works better than the other option of telling and directing.

As humans, we may have strong opinions or vested interests about the issue at stake. But we must realize that as leaders, sometimes we need to ask questions instead of making statements.

What You Get
What are the benefits of showing humility in knowledge? I think they're countless. That's because it shows up in almost every aspect of our lives. It becomes evident in the way we think, in the words we say, and in how we act.

One chief benefit is how it helps to improve and deepen your own knowledge. The more you know, the more you realize how much you don't know. As you become aware of your own drought of knowledge, you begin to appreciate others more. With that appreciation comes the desire to learn from them, no matter how they compare to you – young or old, rich or poor, high or low. As you grow in knowledge, you connect better with people as you seek to add value to them. This helps attract others to you. As I noted in previous chapters, humility is attractive. As you exhibit humility through what you know (or don't know), it attracts good things to you – collaboration, respect, trust, admiration and esteem, among others.

What You Can Do

I believe the first step towards humility in knowledge is an admission that no one knows everything. I don't know all; neither do you. Once that's settled, we can then begin to appreciate the value of dialogue and sharing ideas with others.

Here are a few steps to take towards becoming humble in knowledge:

1. Admit when you make mistakes. It lets others know that you're human after all. Use them as teachable moments; tell others what lessons you learned from your mistakes.

2. Admit verbally that you don't have all the answers when you don't. Then, be intentional about asking others for their opinions and ideas.

3. Don't try to win every argument; this only brings strife. Allow honest debate and let your own assertions be challenged.

4. Assume the role of the follower sometimes; don't think you have to lead every single time. Take the back stage and let others shine.

Readily acknowledging our lack of knowledge and exhibiting the behaviors that back it up ensures that we continue to learn. It helps us be at the receiving end of even more knowledge, as we learn from others.

Apart from knowledge however, the manner in which we receive many other things are equally important in helping us develop humility. How we develop humility in the way we receive is next.

CHAPTER 7
GRACIOUS RECEPTIONS

Examine what is said, not him who speaks.
— Arabic Proverb

When Mariah arrived at her desk that fateful Wednesday morning, the email waiting in her Inbox was the last thing she wanted to see. As she read the email that Mike, her coworker, had sent overnight, she became increasingly agitated. With each word, her anger level went up a few notches. By the time she was done reading the email, the angry explosions in her head had reached astronomical proportions. She couldn't contain herself. She was now officially pissed! She'd blown a gasket and she needed Mike to know exactly how she felt. Her emotions were all over the place.

Mike should have known better!

How dare he send me such a note?!

I'll show him who's the boss!

Mariah hit the *Reply* button and started pounding away furiously at her keyboard. Flowing through her fingers onto the email were all the violent thoughts going through her mind with all of the accompanying negative emotions. She told Mike where to stuff his email and what lake to jump into. When she was done,

157

she looked at her computer screen. SHE HAD WRITTEN IN CAPITAL LETTERS, in **bold**, and changed the font color for many of the explosive words to red. There was a multitude of exclamation points scattered all over the email. She had definitely given him a piece of her mind. She hit *Send*.

Does this sound familiar? Have you or someone you know reacted as violently as this to an email or anything else? I mentioned earlier how humble leaders tend not to take credit; they give it instead. But what happens when you are on the receiving end of something you don't necessarily care for? Something that struck a nerve? What happens when someone pushes your buttons? That's usually the time our ugly side shows up; when the nasty emotions take over.

You and I are emotional beings. Our emotions make up a huge component of who we are. These emotions are the strong driving forces behind almost everything we say or do. But if care is not taken, those emotions can land us in trouble. They can take us places we don't intend on going. There are people who are in prison today because of emotions – theirs or others. There are others who are dead, also because of their emotions or those of others. Many relationships have been destroyed because of emotions. Many more will be destroyed because of emotions. Our emotions tend to drive everything we do.

Your decision to get up from bed this morning and go about your daily business is predicated on your emotions. Most times, you get up and do whatever you do anyway even when you don't feel like it. That's because for many of us, we need the paycheck to meet our financial needs and obligations. And because you're grudgingly doing the work, there's a tendency that you won't put in your very best effort. This comes from how many of us feel about our jobs. We do just enough to slide by.

On the other hand, if you love and enjoy what you do, you can't wait for the day to break for you to get started. You hit the ground running, and you do what you do with joy and excitement. Because you get a lot of satisfaction and fulfillment from what you do, you invest in it. You devote time and effort to learn more, know more and do more. As you do this, excellence is what follows. You become better even though you're already performing at what you thought was your very best.

Our emotions can lead us to success in life, but they can also derail us if we're not careful. This is the reason that the manner in which we deal with our emotions is a crucial aspect of our existence. How we handle our emotions can determine our success or failure in life. It can take us to unimaginable heights in our endeavors. It can relegate us to the lowest levels. The thoughts, words and actions with which we handle our emotions can go a long way to determine our destiny in life.

Keeping Your Minds

Most of us have probably heard someone say, "Sticks and stones may break my bones, but words can never hurt me." I can honestly say categorically that this is a bold-faced lie! Words do hurt, especially when they are intended to do just that – hurt.

Our words have the power to inflict wound and pain on others. They can bring untold emotional agony. One unfortunate fact about words is that once uttered, you can't swallow them back. You can't *un-say* things you have already said. You can choose to retract them. You may even apologize for saying them. But your listeners can never *un-hear* them. Once you say the words, the damage they cause can be irreversible. This is one of the reasons why we should be cautious with our words. And that is especially crucial for those in leadership positions. While this is important when leaders are communicating ideas, it's even more so when responding to hurtful words others say to them or about them.

Some of us are quick to lash out when someone says something we don't like. We challenge their audacity to speak to us in a manner that's not complimentary. We want to let them know that we're better than their hurtful words would suggest, so we return the favor and fling back cruel words at them. We give them a piece of our mind.

In today's culture of ever-present social media, giving a piece of your mind is not limited to words uttered through the vocal cords. Many people have experienced the pain and agony that the 280 characters on Twitter can inflict. The resulting harm is usually beyond anyone's control. The same goes for Facebook, Snapchat and Instagram posts. Once in cyber-space, those online postings take on a life of their own. Even after the original owner may have deleted the entry, copies could still make their way into millions of computers and mobile devices in perpetuity. With email, it's even worse once you hit the *Send* button. The recipient has a permanent record as evidence. Such was the situation described earlier with Mariah.

Mariah's behavior shows what can happen when emotional impulses are not held in check. Such impulses can rage like a wildfire for a brief moment and then die. But they usually leave a trail of destruction in their wake. Regret is usually what follows. Ruined lives and careers may result.

> *Words are like eggs; once they fall and break, you can't put them back together.*
> Yoruba Proverb

People like Mariah have a very low level of an emotional intelligence skill called *Impulse Control*. They're what you would call "hot-headed" or "tempestuous." Low levels of impulse control manifest themselves as explosive behaviors, impulsiveness, anger control problems, and abusiveness, just to name a few.

What is this thing called Impulse Control? In the book, *The EQ Edge*, Steven Stein and Howard Book define it as "the ability to delay an impulse, drive, or temptation to act." It involves "avoiding rash behaviors and decision-making, being composed and being able to put the brakes on angry, aggressive, hostile, and irresponsible behaviors."[1]

One of the key traits that I have noticed with humble people is their high level of impulse control. This shouldn't be a surprise to us, should it? That's because they have a modest view of their own importance. When you have a high view of your importance, you're easily offended when people behave towards you in a manner that lowers that view of your importance. When the arrogant feel slighted, their thoughts could include:

How dare he talk to me like that?

Gracious Receptions

Who does she think she is, to behave
like that towards me?!

It's all about *them* and how your behavior has either demeaned *them* or reduced *their* level of importance. This situation is different with the humble. Because they have a modest view of their own importance, they rarely react impulsively. They don't give a piece of their mind to someone who doesn't care about receiving that piece of their mind. They tend to think before they speak or act. They have good control of their emotions, their words, their behaviors, and use it to their advantage. In general, people with effective impulse control have the capacity to think first, before acting. The relationships they have developed are important to them, so they try not to jeopardize them or break trust with others.[2] They consider all the options, which make them more likely to make better decisions and behave in a responsible manner.

Others like Mariah don't seem to act in their own best interests. More importantly, this impulsive tendency shows up in every area of their lives. They make poor decisions when under pressure, spend money unwisely, and generally have a very low tolerance for frustration. Their responses to frustrating experiences usually end up causing them more anguish.

A number of years ago, my connecting flight at Denver International Airport was cancelled. It was the last flight of the day for the airline into San Francisco. As I was pondering my options, one guy (I'll call him Joe) walked angrily to the airline agent who had just announced the flight cancellation. He started berating her, telling her how important it was for him to get into San Francisco that night. He was completely out of control, cursing and threatening fire and brimstone.

At the end of his temper tantrum, Joe stormed off to look for a hotel in which he would spend the night. Those of us who remained calm were eventually re-booked on other airlines. We were able to make it into San Francisco later that night. But not Joe; he spent the night in Denver, probably still cursing under his breath as he slept. His response to that frustrating experience of flight cancellation prevented him from achieving his goal, which was to arrive in San Francisco that evening.

In most cases, lacking effective impulse control is an ill wind that blows no one any good. You throw tantrums and lash out because you're frustrated for not getting what you want. In the end, you still don't get what you want! In fact, you end up getting the short end of the stick most of the time.

Because of the unprintable things that Mariah sent to Mike, she lost her job after Mike forwarded her email to the company's human resources team. The organization had zero tolerance policy on such things, especially for those who lead teams. Mariah was Mike's manager, and a much better response was required from her no matter how frustrating the situation may have been for her.

My wife once told me about a colleague of hers who quit his job on an impulse. This man had earlier applied for a higher position in the same company. When he found out that he did not make it through the interview process successfully, he resigned immediately and took another job somewhere else. About six months later, he had to quit his new job and return to his former employer. Since his former job had already been given to another person, he had to settle for a much lower position than the one he originally had. In fact, I understand that when he came back, he had to be trained by one of the people that used to report to him. And this was for a position at the level beneath where he was. His impulsive behavior – quitting his job – set him back a few years in his career.

Don't give a piece of your mind to someone who doesn't care about receiving that piece of your mind.

Let's talk about you for a moment. Are your impulsive behaviors causing you to lose and miss out on better things in life? How do you respond to frustrating and stressful situations? How effective are you at controlling your impulses? Like most components of emotional intelligence, impulse control can be improved with coaching and guided practice. You can begin by following a simple 3-step process – *Pause, Ponder, Proceed.*

Pause – Stop and resist your initial instinctive urge to act right away. Just do nothing for a moment and allow the rational side of your brain enough time for processing. Research says it takes about six to eight seconds for this to happen. This may be difficult at the beginning especially if you've become used to reacting quickly. But with practice, you will get better at it.

Ponder – Take time to think and process what's going on – consider your options. Ask yourself, "Does this situation call for immediate action?" Even if immediate action is required, it probably doesn't need to be faster than the eight seconds your brain needs, to come up with more reasonable solutions.

> *A fool's displeasure is known at once, but whoever ignores an insult is sensible.*
> King Solomon

Proceed – Go ahead and pick the best response for the situation. The best response usually does not involve insulting the other person or doing something that could destroy the relationship with them.

As you go through these three steps repeatedly, you should begin to see some results. A word of caution here – please don't expect overnight results. But you must be consistent in practicing these steps even when it seems there's no change right away. It takes some time to change those impulses that were developed over many years. If you don't see any improvements after about six months of consistent practice, you may want to reach out for professional help before it's too late. A lot in your future may depend on it.

A Gift Worth Receiving

For many of us, receiving negative feedback without being defensive can be a very difficult endeavor. We typically don't like someone telling us what we're not doing well. It bruises our egos. That's true even when we already know that we have opportunities to improve in those areas. Despite that, we can still behave in ways that seek to protect our self-esteem.

Years ago, I had a colleague who was always quick to volunteer for tasks and also commit voluntarily to specific deadlines for the completion of those tasks. But most of the time, he wouldn't deliver on his promises. After noticing this pattern with him on a few occasions, I decided to speak to him about it. To do this, I asked him into a private meeting. I told him how much I loved his enthusiasm for getting things done, but wondered if he was taking on too much at the same time. I gave him three instances over the previous year when he had missed deadlines that he committed to, without trying to re-negotiate those deadlines. I explained how this could affect his credibility as a person.

To his credit, his first response was to thank me for taking the time to discuss this with him. But everything after that went downhill. I could easily tell from his body language that he did not like what had just happened. During our half-hour discussion, he used the phrase, "I take an exception to that" at least twice, while referring to the specific examples in which I thought he did not follow through. At one point, he actually asked me what right I had to come to him with what he called "accusations that had no basis." And he was absolutely correct. I had no right. So, I apologized to him for bringing the issue up and left the room. As I walked away, I knew he wasn't the kind of person you'd want to stick your neck out to rescue even if it was obvious that he was about to fall over a cliff. There was no way I would ever approach him to discuss anything along the same lines again.

Whoever loves discipline loves knowledge, but whoever hates correction is stupid.
Hebrew Proverb

After that experience with my colleague, I started wondering about how many times I must have had a similar attitude towards someone who was trying to give me some much-needed and useful feedback. I quickly lost count! I knew I had to turn over a new leaf.

We all have areas of our lives in which we don't want others sniffing around. Those are the untouchables. We know that we struggle in those areas. We may even already be beating ourselves up concerning them. But woe betide whoever dare point out those weaknesses! We already know about them, and we're trying to deal with them on our own. We just don't want them exposed to others. We prefer to continue struggling with it under the cover of obscurity. It could be a personality trait that rubs others the wrong way, or an annoying habit we've unknowingly picked up but is now difficult to shake. Sometimes, we just don't want to be seen as inadequate in areas of life we consider important. This reminds me of an experience that Linda (not her real name) told me about.

After her husband shared some feedback with her about some areas that he felt they were struggling in their marriage, Linda got very angry and walked away. She went through the house and got busy with numerous household chores for several hours. She was just too angry to talk. She confessed to me, "I don't like being told where I am falling short in the most important relationship I have. It's definitely wounded pride on my part."[3] But she also agreed that, "putting more distance between us doesn't solve any problems; it creates more. Then we both have to put more effort into working through any issues." When I asked about how she could have responded differently, she said, "I could have remained calm and asked my husband to explain why he felt the way he did about each of the issues. I could have shared my perspective with him and then talked through the differences in our perspectives to reach a mutual understanding where we could both be happy."

You and I can take a cue from those last few comments from Linda when we're confronted with feedback we don't necessarily like. Instead of getting defensive or blaming the observer, we could try to understand the other person's perspective. While this is by no means easy because of the way it bruises our ego, it's still our best initial approach. To become better at receiving these types of feedback, I have found three things that can help: ask for it, avoid mere lip service, and say "Thank you."

Ask for It

Early in my career, I was one of those who responded very poorly to receiving unwanted feedback. After some reflection, I began to see that the feedback I was receiving was to my benefit. I realized that those giving me the feedback were not doing it just to frustrate or spite me. They were doing it in my best interest, but it was still difficult for me to receive. Some of it really hurt! So, to take the sting out, I decided to go on the offensive. I would ask trusted colleagues to be honest and to tell me what I wasn't doing well.

Years ago, as a project manager, I started the practice of asking for specific feedback from my project teams, customers, vendors and all others that I had contact with, in the course of executing a project. At the end of each project, I would send each of these people a questionnaire to provide me feedback on how I performed as I led the project. Intentionally, I made sure that the very last question on the questionnaire was, "What could I have done better? Tell me one thing you think I should have done differently."

By asking this particular question, I was giving them permission to provide me with the kind of feedback that could help me get better. I have found this to be ver helpful. This is especially true in situations in which they had something to say but were reluctant to do so. It also removed the sting that I would otherwise have felt from an unsolicited feedback. Over the years, this practice has helped me to become more gracious in receiving feedback, even when I did not ask for it.

Whether it's in the workplace or in our personal relationships, adopting this approach can help us become more gracious in receiving pointed feedback. Best-selling author, Kevin Kruse posted the following on his LinkedIn page on October 9, 2017:

> I had just sold my company to Kenexa, where I became a VP reporting to the CEO. On my very first day, it was a company quarterly meeting. The CEO gave a speech at the front of the room. As the new guy I was "hiding" in the back.
>
> The CEO finished his speech and came right up to me. "How'd I do?"
>
> My boss, on my first day at work, was asking me for feedback on his speech.
>
> "Great, Rudy. You did great."
>
> "What could I do better?" he asked.
>
> "I really thought it was great."

Gracious Receptions

And then he did it. He asked, "If you HAD to come up with just one thing that I could do to be better next time, what would it be?"

He forced me to say the one thing I really thought but wasn't going to tell him.

If you REALLY want feedback on your next presentation, sales call, leadership style, whatever...just ask...

"...If I absolutely HAD to make just one change, what should it be?"

It stings me every time, but I'm better for it.

If you adopt this attitude of truly wanting and asking for feedback on areas you can improve, you will be better for it.

No Lip Service

Whether solicited or not, receiving negative feedback is not easy. Lashing out or becoming defensive is our natural response. But if you go on the offensive and ask for it as I noted above, ensure that you truly mean it.

Don't pay lip service to your request for true constructive feedback. Leaders especially need to be careful when they ask for feedback. Those you lead will know if you're a phony right away. I was once part of a team where the leadership talked about having an open-door policy, and encouraged team members to have the courage to speak up. But when people followed through and provided feedback, any voice of dissent was quickly silenced. It looked like when they asked for feedback, they were only expecting kudos and pats on the back for what they've done well. The result was that many who had real and helpful but unflattering feedback kept quiet and said nothing.

Just Say 'Thank You'

Irrespective of how ridiculous the feedback seems, or how angry you may be on receiving it, your immediate response should be to simply thank the person for having the courage to speak up. This is especially important if they're not in a position of authority over you. Thank them for their courage. Let them know how much you appreciate the fact that they have your best interests at heart. Next, take a few days to think about it, and if necessary, approach them later to ask clarifying questions. As you do this, you are demonstrating humility, showing them that you are coach-able, and will listen.

Whether you realize it or not, we all have blind spots. You have yours and I have mine. We need the help of those around us to help discover what they are. As they share their discoveries with you, they're giving you a gift – a gift that you would do well to receive. That gift may come in packages we don't really care for – tone, attitude or even the words used. But we need to learn to see them for what they truly are – gifts meant to help us become better. Walter Hooker told me that "when humility hears feedback or criticism, it says, 'This is meant to help me and make me better', regardless of the vessel. Most of the time, the vessel delivers it the wrong way. If you don't respond with humility, you may just be hearing the attitude with which the vessel is delivering it."[4]

Even if their intent is to hurt you, they may not realize that they are unintentionally adding value to you. The value-add can come in the form of learning to receive the feedback with humility. It could also help you discover blind spots that you've not seen before. When you choose to view the criticism positively, your stocks have no place to go but up, but this can be very tough to deal with if the critic's voice is the only one amongst a chorus of praise.

Dealing with the Anti-Accolade
What do you do when situations arise in which the unwanted critical feedback comes from only one or two sources? It becomes even more difficult to receive when those lone voices are coming in the midst of praises and accolades from many others. When you receive approval and commendations for doing something, it can be difficult to listen to those who are telling you that you can do better with that same thing. In this case, you can easily justify your decision to reject these lone voices of dissent. You dig your heels in, discount the feedback and decide that something must be wrong with them. How can they be the only ones seeing

something wrong? They must be jealous of your success! If not, what other reasons could there be, for them to take a position that is opposite of almost every other person's?

An experience that my good friend, Femi Awodele, shared with me drives this point home. Here's what he told me:

> Many years ago, before social media became ubiquitous as it is today, I was a columnist for an online forum called NigeriaWorld. Within a short time, my writings had a huge following and I was receiving commendations and letters of praise from people in different parts of the globe. Then suddenly, I received a note from someone in Pennsylvania, who said, among other things, "Young man, your columns are too long. You should reduce the number of pages so people don't quit reading half-way. Also, try and proofread your copies after writing them, so you can catch your grammar and spelling mistakes."

> My initial response was defensive, and in anger, I replied to his note in a nasty and sarcastic manner. I told him that despite the mistakes, God was using my writing and people were getting value from it because I continued to receive a large number of positive feedback and comments. The funny thing was that he wasn't the first person to point this out. My own wife had been telling me the same thing, and I refused to listen.

> It took me about two years to eventually realize and consider that they were right all along. When I did, I followed the man's recommendations – I reduced the length of my articles and started taking time to read over my pieces before sending them out for publication. I began to discover many mistakes and was able to correct them prior to publication. I also wrote another article in which I detailed how the man corrected me and how I had initially spurned his correction. In that

article, I stated that even though I saw value in what he said, the way he said it so rubbed me the wrong way, that it dictated my initial response to him.

Since that experience, I've tried to be open to being corrected and not allow it to get to me personally, irrespective of how the correction came.[5]

My hope is that we can all put in the effort to continually receive with humility, the critical feedback that we're given, especially in the midst of accolades. This doesn't mean that all such feedback will be useful to us, but we owe it to ourselves not to allow those initial, instinctive and automatic reactions (which tend to be negative most of the time), to dictate our ultimate response.

If you have a tendency to respond negatively, those giving you feedback will be very hesitant to do so in the future. The implications of this are that you may be cutting off forever, the flow of insights that could help you navigate blind spots and avoid mistakes in your life. Even if you take pride in doing things with excellence, there are times when you will make mistakes. You need others to help you spot them.

Short of Perfection
There are many people who take pleasure in doing a good job. They put all of their effort and mental energy into focusing on delivering excellent and quality work anytime they have the opportunity. These people are at the other end of the spectrum that Femi Awodele described in the last section. They pour over every detail, dotting every *"i"* and crossing every *"t."* Their passion is to approach perfection as closely as possible. Oddly enough, these are the kinds of people who are also more likely to be offended when someone else points out what they could have done better.

The sting of this type of feedback is stronger for them because they thought they had covered all their bases. For many in this category, lashing out at the person who gives the feedback is more likely their way of beating themselves up for missing what they thought their diligence should have taken care of. Some of them react this way because, subconsciously it diminishes their self-worth. They think they're less than who they are just because of that one miscue. I know this for a fact because I was like that. Over the last decade, however, I've come to realize that my self-esteem doesn't depend on whether or not I do something well. It lies in who I am in the One who created me and gave me life. I have realized that my talents (and the talents I don't have) are gifts I've been given. And you don't earn gifts. They're given. So, I've chosen to work on growing in the areas I can, and leave the rest to the One who loves me just as I am.

This is the same approach Kim has decided to take. She wrote to tell me how much she dislikes not doing things well and how much it stings when people point out her failures. She admitted to being "a recovering perfectionist, but learning to be a woman of excellence instead." She continued, "I tend to put too much of my identity and self-worth into what other people think. Some criticisms have crushed me and cause me to go the other way or make a strong mental note to never do that again. Other times, it has caused me to grow." She concluded that now, she "chooses to evaluate and grow, and not worry about others' opinions or my self-worth."[6]

You can choose to adopt the same tactic as Kim. Instead of trying to be perfect, you can strive for excellence. Rather than evaluating your worth through the lenses of negative feedback or your miscues, you can see yourself just as God made you – wonderfully complex![7] To be clear, this is not an excuse to revel in mediocrity. It's a realization and the acceptance of the fact that while you are good at some things, you're also not good at some other things. You simply cannot be good at everything. You can work hard to achieve excellence in what you're good at, and leverage the talents of others for those areas in which you're not very good. As you do this, you're paying less attention to your view of your own importance. You are becoming humble.

In My Defense
In some situations, you receive feedback in the form of an attack on your actions, motives and personality. This is not the helpful

kind of feedback that we have just discussed. We're talking about being falsely attacked and accused. The obvious intentions here are to hurt and harm you. These assaults may be in response to decisions you've made or the ones you refused to make. In these situations, what do you do? How do you respond to unjustified attacks on your actions, motives, and intentions? To be honest, I think this is a very tough one to deal with.

It reminds me of something that happened several millennia ago during the formative years of Israel as a nation, when they were being led out of slavery by Moses. As the leader of this massive exodus of people from Egypt to the promised land, there was a tremendous amount of pressure on Moses. Several times along the way, some people would challenge his authority to lead, especially when they faced problems.

In one of those attacks against Moses, he was criticized for marrying someone from another country. Zipporah, Moses' wife

Your self-esteem is not dependent on whether or not you do something well.

was from Cush, a region south of Ethiopia. She was not born a Jew, and some people took exception to that. The interesting thing about this attack was that Moses was not recently married at the time this accusation was leveled against him. He had been married to Zipporah long before he was even called to go rescue the Israelites from slavery, so this was not new. Why did it suddenly become an issue during the journey?

I think it was just another attempt by those who disliked his leadership to find one more excuse to berate him. When you don't like someone, you find ways to complain about even the most mundane or irrelevant things. One can only imagine how long that resentment against Moses had been brewing before it finally reared its ugly head. It was nothing more than another way for them to attack Moses and claim that he was unfit to lead the people.

To make matters worse, the instigators of this attack were his own brother and sister. Aaron and Miriam were the ringleaders of this rebellious outrage against Moses. What kind of sibling rivalry

Gracious Receptions

was this? Maybe they just didn't like Zipporah. Maybe it was because they had had no say, in Moses' decision to marry her. By the time they met her for the first time, she was already their sister-in-law. That was because Moses met and married her while he was in exile from Egypt. I can only imagine the cold receptions she must have endured from them each time there was a family get-together.

What did Moses do? How did he respond to this unnecessary and unjust attack him? With absolute humility! There was no record that he responded harshly towards his siblings. He allowed God to fight the battle for him.[8]

As with Moses, there are times when an attack on a leader has nothing to do with the actual accusations being leveled against them. It could just be another avenue to find fault and pass blame. By questioning his choice of wife, they were casting aspersions on his leadership and decision-making capabilities. These types of attacks are meant to hit strongly at the core of who you are. When this happens, some us respond in kind – we attack them back. The rest of us may be more reasonable, and we respond with facts to dispute the accusations. That's what I would have done had I found myself in this situation. My natural instinct would have been to vigorously defend myself by laying out the facts. There's nothing more frustrating than an attack that is unjustified, which is designed purely to demean who you are.

In 2017, a huge debate started in the United States about immigration. The president was threatening to build hundreds of miles of wall along the southern border to curb the entry of illegal immigrants. Well-meaning people took up strong positions on both sides of the debate. In response to what President Trump then called "an invasion of criminals," we saw an increase in hate crimes against people who look like they may have come from beyond the country's southern border. Some people were assaulted or verbally attacked. Immigration officials were called to arrest people who turned out to be citizens or legal residents. Many of these attacks were driven by fear and anger against people who did not deserve such. Some have referred to this as racism, but I think it's a little deeper than that. I think it's the sorry human state that wants to believe that we are better than others;

that we are more important than they are. It's our own view of our importance when compared to others that drives us to such inhumane behaviors. I know this for a fact because this is not limited to the United States. Similar things are happening in other places around the world.

While this was going on in America, something that at the surface may seem different was happening in my native country of Nigeria. It's really not different, though, because it's driven by the same attitude and view of our own importance when compared to others. There's a part of the country that began clamoring for separation from the rest of the nation. Many of these efforts were being championed by some Nigerians in diaspora who had no clue as to the level of damage this would do. A similar attitude triggered the Nigerian Civil War in the late 1960s. Over one million people died during that period of unnecessary bloodshed, but it seems we never learn from history.

Whether we call it racism in the United States, tribalism in Nigeria, or something else in other countries, it's the same thing. It's the same natural human condition and tendency that seeks to elevate self above others. It has to do with our own view of our importance when compared to others. We push others down in order to elevate ourselves. We make others feel inferior to establish our own superiority.

Eleanor Roosevelt was reputed to have said, "No one can make you feel inferior without your consent," and I agree with her. The purpose of the unjustified attacks on you and your motives is to belittle you and make you feel less than who you really are. The consent you give to such behaviors is your responses to them. I think that when you respond in kind – or with anger – you're giving a stamp of approval to their behavior. Their goal when they ridicule you is simply to get you riled up, and when you display the slightest irritation or anger in response to their behavior, you have helped them achieve their purpose. You've made their day. They've won.

However, when you and I make the conscious choice to see their behavior differently, it loses its sting. When you know who you are and understand what you're worth, no one can diminish

Gracious Receptions

your value by what they say or do to you. You are a creation of value. You are created on purpose by a God who loves you and who knows how much you are worth. You're priceless in His sight, and nothing anyone can do or say can put even a smudge on you. Once you know whose you are, you know who you are. Always remember that.

Thankfully, what we receive from others is not always unwanted feedback or attacks on our personalities and motives. Other times, we're offered good things that can add value to us. The way in which we respond to, and receive these, are equally important.

Help Not Needed
Larry and his wife, Shellie lived a quiet life with their two kids. Larry was the sole bread-winner; his wife stayed at home to care for the children. His income was just enough to support them. Because their needs were simple, this was no problem. That is, until he got hurt on the job, and was unable to work. Suddenly, the family wondered how they would survive.

As is customary, many people from their church visited the family to see how Larry was doing. Amongst these was an old retired couple, Mark and Lucy. Like everyone, they told Larry and Shellie to let them know if they needed anything. But three days later, they returned and Mark said, "We've been praying for you, and we had this strong impression to come back and offer you this. Larry, since I'm retired and you're injured and can't work, how about I go to work for you? I will find a job and work, with the entire income coming to you so your family can be taken care of. And I can do this until you're able to get back on your feet."

No one can make you feel inferior without your consent.
Eleanor Roosevelt

The first instinct from Larry and Shellie was to say, "No, we can handle it. We don't need the help." It's not difficult to see that they really did *need* the help, even if they might not have wanted it. However, this couple was humble enough to receive the offer of help with no strings attached.

175

Larry and Shellie swallowed whatever pride could have prevented them from receiving much-needed help. Many of us can learn from, and take a cue from them. From personal experience, I know many Americans who would most likely decline such an offer of help. We are raised to be independent and self-sufficient. We don't want anybody doing anything for us, especially people we don't know. Even when such assistance is coming from family members or others that we know well, I've seen many people refuse the offer of help. We don't want to owe people. Or maybe we just don't want them to *own* us. We want no handouts. We feel an obligation towards reciprocating a good deed, if we receive one.

As a result, we don't ask for help even when it's sorely needed. And if someone sees the need and offers to help, we decline. I think this comes from a place of arrogance. Yes, you read that exactly as I intended it. It is because of pride that we decline offers of help when it's obvious that we desperately need it. I've even heard people use words like *pride* or *proud* as reasons for not accepting help. Even in cases when we don't use these words, it can still be clear to others that they're the reasons we refuse help. That was the case with me not too long ago.

In recent years, I have been part of a mission team that my church sends to different remote places in Africa. Usually, in order to cover the travel expenses, each team member is encouraged to raise and solicit funds. You do this by asking friends and family to support you both prayerfully and financially. Personally, I have difficulty with asking for financial support. I just don't like asking people for money, so when the next opportunity for the mission trip arrived, I decided it would be easier to simply not go with the team. To me, that was better than going through the stress of raising funds for the trip. This was despite the fact that I know giving others the opportunity to support me financially is good for them. It helps them be a part of the good work we do while on the mission trip. There is also a great blessing in giving and helping others. I know all this, yet I've always been sheepish about asking for others to provide the needed support.

So, when I kept saying I wasn't going with the team simply because I did not want to ask people for money, the team leader

Gracious Receptions

one day held me by the shoulders, looked me straight in the eye and said, "Sunday, you just need to swallow your pride and ask for help!" Ouch! That stung on so many different levels that I couldn't find the appropriate words to describe it. But after much reflection, I realized that he was right. I simply needed to swallow my pride and ask for help. The proud don't ask for help. The humble do, especially when it's really needed or (like in this case), when asking for help will actually benefit those who help.

A few years ago, I was facilitating a seminar for project managers in Las Vegas, Nevada. On the second day of the seminar, we started discussing the emotional intelligence skill called *Social Responsibility*, which I alluded to earlier. In short, it addresses one's willingness to help others. During that seminar, the discussion soon came around to how people respond to offers of help and other such gestures. Then, I asked the participants, "What are the reasons why you may not accept an offer of help from someone, even when you really need it?"

Many of the responses were due to pride. I heard some of the participants say things like,

> I'm a proud person.

> I can't accept their offer of help.

> I'll figure it out on my own.

Since then, I've asked this same question at every emotional intelligence seminar I've done. Most of the responses are similar each time.

While many of us may not go around hat-in-hand, begging for help, I think it behooves us to learn to display enough humility by accepting such help when offered. Those who are offering do so because of two simple premises: they see an unmet need; and they believe that they are in a position to do something about it.

Do you know what happens when you refuse offers of help from willing sources? Depending on your relationship with the people offering help, your connection with them can become strained or damaged. They may become frustrated or confused,[9] especially if this has become a consistent pattern with you. Your rejection could be taken personally and your relationship with them could become unhealthy.[10] Some may even offer help because they have wronged you in the past, and this is their attempt to mend fences,[11] a way to apologize for the pain they have caused you. When you continually refuse help, they will eventually stop offering it,[12] and this may come at a time when you may be desperate and hoping for any form of help from anyone.

Finally, and more importantly, when you refuse their offer of help, you may be denying them the opportunity to tap into one of the greatest sources of joy known to mankind. Studies have shown that being others-centered – helping *Learn to be gracious* people in need – is a major contributor *in accepting help.* to living a happy and fulfilled life. By refusing help when you need it, you may be taking away their chance to experience the joy that comes from giving and of becoming a blessing to you.

So, instead of saying, "No, thank you" to offers of help, learn to be gracious in accepting help, knowing that in doing so, you will be helping not only yourselves, but also your benefactors in ways you could not have imagined. Nevertheless, what's even more important is seeking and asking for help when it's really needed.

Not Looking

While lack of humility can show up in not accepting help that is offered, it can also be displayed in not seeking the help that is desperately needed. In many cases, this shows up in the resistance to seek help for correcting damaging behaviors. We all have behaviors that we can do without. That's because no one is perfect. Sometimes, those negative behaviors can be very damaging to the relationships that are most important to us. It reminds me of the story of Sam and Jen.

Within a few months of being married, Sam began to notice some behaviors from Jen that constantly troubled him. While she was kind and generous to most people who knew her, she was also very controlling, especially with those closest to her. Things had to be done her way; if not, she would get visibly angry and start throwing tantrums. In this state, she would sometimes say very hurtful things to her husband, even things that were untrue. This was what made the situation intolerable for Sam. How could she knowingly saying things that she knew to be false just to hurt him when she was angry? He knew this was what was happening because that's what she would tell him she had done, after cooling down from her rage.

Once she had cooled down, she would apologize. But then, a few day later, it would happen again, and the cycle of cooling down and apologizing would repeat itself. After a few years, Sam realized that despite Jen's repeated apologies, nothing was changing in her behavior. He decided that they needed help. He wanted them to see a therapist, or for Jen to at least talk to one of the trusted leaders in their church who could help her. But Jen wouldn't hear of it. Yes, she knew she had a problem, but it's her problem; not anyone else's (she thought), so she's the one to fix it. She told her husband that she did not want their dirty laundry aired in public out for someone else to see.

Over the next two decades, Sam grew increasingly weary from all the emotional trauma and could barely take it anymore. However, he did not want their children torn apart, so he continued to endure. Immediately after their last child graduated from college, he filed for divorce. He had hung on long enough just for the sake of his children, but he finally called it quits after twenty-eight years of marriage. Their friends were shocked. They did not know what had been going on all these years because Jen did not agree to seek help, and Sam never told anyone about all the emotional abuse he was enduring. The result was a broken marriage.

Do you know the damage that is being done to your most important relationships because of your behaviors? Can you determine the extent of the damage you're causing? Jen did not realize the degree to which her destructive behaviors were affecting the relationship she valued the most. More importantly, her view of her own self-importance blinded her to the toll her behaviors were taking on her family. It eventually led to the collapse of her marriage. Her arrogance in not wanting to seek help for her hurtful behaviors eventually led her to sabotage the most important relationship in her life.

As I stated before, none of us is perfect. But when the worst of your tendencies and actions deal continual blows to the psyche of the people you cherish the most, you risk destroying your relationships with them. You must choose to seek help in those areas. Refusing to seek help, and continuing to think you can fix the problem when experience has shown that you cannot, is just another symptom of your arrogance. It is a sign of your high view of your own importance. That's definitely not the way to live because we each need strong, loving relationships to live life to the fullest. It is my belief that we truly start to live when we choose to become dead to our own view of how important we are. Our life begins at the funeral where we bury our pride and pointless sense of self-sufficiency.

Praise-shy
How do you typically respond to compliments, commendations, admirations, or praises in public? Do you embrace them or recoil in horror? I heard from some people who have learned to receive adulations with modesty. Jacquie wrote to tell me that she tries to "accept the praise or compliment and not dismiss it or not say it was nothing, but to just appreciate it in the spirit it was given."[13] Another person told me that she likes it but sometimes, she feels weird about it because she doesn't want others to "feel left out."[14] But many of those who responded to my questions about this seem to not like it that much. When praised, there are those who do not like the attention it brings. They prefer to blend into the background. At first glance, it may seem that many of us shy away from receiving a praise or compliment out of humility. But through an encounter that I had in 2013, I learned that sometimes, knowing how to receive praises, compliments, and recognitions could be an even more significant sign of humility.

It was at the conclusion of a fund-raising event for a mission team that my church was sending to Kenya. I had helped to organize the event and more than fifty other volunteers were involved. At the end of the program, I was supposed to give the vote of thanks to everyone who worked to make that event a reality, especially the various team leaders who had worked

Gracious Receptions

directly with me.

As I was being introduced to take the microphone, the pastor who was responsible for leading the team, and on whose behalf, I had organized the event, jumped in and snatched the microphone from me. Instinctively, I knew what he was going to do; he was going to talk about me and thank me for organizing the event. Almost immediately, I thought to myself, "That's not a good idea!" So, what did I do? I started to playfully wrestle with him to give me back the microphone right there on the stage, with several hundreds of people watching. After a few unsuccessful attempts to get the microphone from him, I finally gave in. He then proceeded to confirm my fears about what he was going to do. He heaped praises on me and the work I had done to put the event together. As he spoke, I thought it would have been a much better experience if the ground had opened up and swallowed me whole!

I strongly dislike such attention. I do not like to be recognized and commended, especially while I'm standing right there! I don't mind it being done while I'm absent; I just do not enjoy experiencing it. Those were the times when I really blushed; thankfully, no one could tell because my skin color hides it very well! I know that this may seem silly to some of you, but there are many people like me who do not like being recognized publicly.

When being praised in public, Melba told me she typically feels embarrassed. She said, "I overthink it. I start to wonder; does everyone agree with the compliment? Do they think I'm fake? Did the person really mean the nice things they said?"[15] Rebecca confessed to me by saying, "The one compliment I do not know how to take is the one where people come up to me and say, 'You're so talented! I could never do what you do!'" She concluded, "Complimenting me on a gift I didn't earn, that allowed me to do something they couldn't do, is like complimenting Michael Jordan for being tall!"[16] For Nair, she just doesn't like being the center of attention,[17] which usually happens when she's recognized while others are present. On one such occasion when she was recognized for doing exceptional work in front of her leadership team, she was so nervous that she could barely speak. Some of us can probably identify with this.

NOTHING HIGHER

According to the results of a research study[18] published in the *Journal of Experimental Social Psychology*, people with low self-esteem have the most difficulty accepting compliments. I know some of you are probably thinking, "Woah, woah, wait a minute! How can shying away from compliments be due to low self-esteem?" I know. That was also my initial reaction to the findings of this study. I don't think that my self-esteem is low, but I still feel uncomfortable receiving compliments. That may also be the case for many of you. But this is what the result of this particular study says. For those with low self-esteem, you may want to invest in resources that could help you tackle this or identify what your core values are.

In addition, it's been found that shying away from accepting praise could be one of the "side-effects" of being humble. As you're already aware from all that we've already covered in this book, humility leads to many positive outcomes. However, accepting compliments can sometimes be accompanied by feelings of superiority complex, rather than a graceful acknowledgment. This may explain why people who are humble may find it difficult to accept praises and compliments. I think each one of us must evaluate this for ourself. Do you recoil from recognition because of genuine humility or self-esteem issues? On the other hand, do you embrace such compliments because they feed your ego, or do you accept them as mere acknowledgements of how others see you? Only you can tell. You must be honest in your self-evaluation.

For those of us who recoil from this experience, the uneasiness we feel when receiving compliments may never go away, but we can still learn to accept these praises without allowing the awkwardness to show up in our behaviors, such as trying to wrestle away the microphone from someone! Instead of grabbing or pulling at someone in order to avoid compliments coming your way, you can simply accept them, knowing that these are just expressions of the positive regard that they have for you. That's what I have tried to do over the last few years to overcome the clumsiness I feel when being recognized publicly.

Gracious Receptions

No Swollen Heads Here

Being recognized for accomplishments is a huge deal to some people. In fact, it's such a huge deal that they can't wait to brag about the recognition. But sometimes, their boasting could lead to their bubble being burst by others. That's what happened to Louis.

Louis was the manager of a small team of service engineers. This team provided service to their company's customers spread over a huge geographic portion of the state in which the team was located. At the end of each year, the entire technical team across the country would come together at the company's headquarters to celebrate achievements over the past year and give awards to the best performers from each of the four regions of the country.

During one year's award recognitions, Louis was recognized as the best from his region. This was unusual because the awards usually go to the service engineers, and not their managers. At the after-party following the presentation of the awards, Louis went around boasting to anyone that would listen, about how his performance as a manager was so good that he was recognized with an award that should have gone to someone not at his level. He would brag about how he was better than the service engineers in his region despite

Accepting compliments could sometimes be accompanied by feelings of superiority complex.

the fact that it had been a few years since he operated at that level. After observing the way in which he carried on bragging, his boss (who was the regional manager) called him and Simon into his office. Simon was one of the service engineers on Louis' team.

Once the door was closed behind them in the office, Walter looked at Louis and said, "Do you realize that the award we gave you was actually meant for Simon?" Both Louis and Simon were shocked.

"What?!" Simon exclaimed. "Why wasn't it given to me then?"

Walter turned to Simon and said, "After we received your one-month notice of resignation last week, we decided that we would not be giving you the award as planned."

Simon was beyond belief. "Why?! Isn't the award for past performance? My resignation should have had nothing to do with whether it was given to me or not."

Walter looked at Simon with empathy and explained. "Yes, the award is for your exceptional performance over this past year. But we also see it as a motivation for you to continue performing at that level. Since you're leaving the company, we decided not to give it to you because you won't be here to continue that level of performance for the organization. And because we received your resignation so close to when we'd be presenting the awards, we decided to just give it to your boss instead."

Then he turned to Louis, "I thought you should know why you received the award, so think twice before you continue to boast about receiving an award that was not really yours to begin with."

Louis was stunned. His illusions about why he got the award were totally shattered. He left the room completely deflated.

Here's what I know. Humble people do not feel the need to boast about what they've achieved. Neither do they use the opportunity to act superior to, or look down on others, because of their own accomplishments. Those who have great character acknowledge and celebrate the achievement of others, even if it's at their own expense. They don't engage in talk or behavior that puts others down.

There's another reason for not getting puffed up. Many times, we achieve success because of our natural gifts and abilities. Yes, you may have worked hard to develop and hone those talents into strengths, but remember that it all started with the natural talent. And you don't take credit for those. You *can't* take credit for them. You can only be grateful. Your natural talents are endowments from the Creator, and He gives each one of us different talents as He chooses. As John Wooden said, "Talent is God-given. Be humble." Your talents may be different from mine, but that doesn't make mine better than or superior to yours. Each talent is a gift that is unique to the recipient. Even the expression of the same talent in any two people may not be the same. So, who am I to allow this to get into my head? Who are you to use the gifts that you have received to belittle someone who has not

Gracious Receptions

received such a gift?

We all have strengths and weaknesses. My responsibility is to first identify, then nurture and develop my natural talents into strengths that I can use in positive ways to help those around me. I believe that's your responsibility also, with your own natural talents. I like the way Becky puts it. She said, "Talent is an indication of where you should focus your energies. But talent, in and of itself, will not accomplish anything. It just gets your toe in the door. In fact, all talent does is indicate which door you should stick your toe in. The rest depends on hard work, consistency, insight, study and persistence."[17] Unfortunately, there are people who choose not to work hard to develop their talents. Such talents are wasted on them as they let these rust away.

In February of 2019, just as a new season of Major League Baseball was about to start in North America, I read a brief interview given by one of the most talented ballplayers of his generation. Yasiel Puig had played the first six years of his career in the major leagues with the Los Angeles Dodgers. In December 2018, he was traded to another team, the Cincinnati Reds. In the interview, Puig confessed that he did not work hard while he was in Los Angeles because he was still under a contract. With the one-year contract he has with the Reds for the 2019 season, he said, "Now, I think I'll work hard than any year of my life."[19] By his own admission, he's been lazy for most of his time in Los Angeles. He had the talent, but did not utilize it to its full potential.

Could the same thing be said of you? Do you have talents that you're allowing to rot away? When will you take the bull by the horns and begin to live to your potential? I sure hope the answer to that last question is *Immediately!* Just as not taking credit for your talents shows humility, I also think each of us have the responsibility to develop our talents into strengths that can be used to benefit others. Using our talents to the best of our abilities is one way we show the humility in gratitude for those talents. We do this instead of obsessing over others' talents that we may think are better than ours.

ꓠOTHING ꓱIGHER

My Pleasure

Anytime you go into a Chick-fil-A restaurant or go through one of their drive-through lanes, the response from any of their associates is always the same whenever you say the words, "Thank you!" You will always get "My pleasure!" in response from them. It's the same every time, so much that it has become an easily predictable response for those of us who patronize them frequently. In fact, one of their trainers told me that each associate has been trained to respond that way anytime they hear "thank you." One day, I decided to do something that I hoped would throw them completely off their game.

After receiving my order at the drive-through window, instead of saying the customary "thank you," I decided to go with, "I appreciate you!" On another occasion, I said, "I'm grateful." But these did not do the trick! Each time, the person still responded with "My pleasure!" It seems they are conditioned to respond that way no matter what you say.

Many of us have a similar type of conditioning. When someone thanks you for doing something for them, how do you typically respond? Just think about it! What's the first response that pops into your mind when thanked for something you've done? This is supposed to be a no-brainer, right? But it's not! For people in most parts of the world, a simple "you're welcome" is the typical reply. In the United States however, I have since learned that the responses could vary wildly:

Don't mention it.	Sure thing!
It's nothing.	No problem!
You bet!	It's my pleasure.
Glad to help out.[20]	No, thank you!
Thank God!	That's how I roll!

There are different reasons why we respond whichever way we do, and many of us may not even know why we respond that way. We just do. More often than not, this is rooted in who we are, how we were raised, or the culture in which we grew up. For example,

Gracious Receptions

Vivien says "Thank God!" in response because she believes "it is God that makes it possible for me to be in the position of giving that helping hand."[21] Someone else wrote to tell me that helping others is motivating for them, and that they are truly glad to help.[22]

Talent is God-given;
be humble.
Fame is man-given;
be grateful.
Conceit is self-given;
be careful.
John Wooden

Another person said they wanted the person thanking them to know that what they did was a genuine gesture.[23] Jacquie agrees that "it's easy to dismiss words of thanks, but if it is given, I want to make the other person aware that I appreciate their thanks."[24] On the other hand, Hope Valentine is usually filled with awe that "people would have the courtesy to say 'Thank You' and that they don't feel a sense of entitlement."[25] So, there are a variety of reasons for why we respond the way we do. But when we are quick to pass off a genuine, sincerely offered expression of appreciation, it could show pride lurking around within us.

Wait! What?!

If you take a close look, some of these responses seem to diminish the impact of the contributions for which the thanks are being offered. Often, it is in an attempt to be humble that we try to minimize the positive value or effects of what was done. But I don't think this shows humility.

When someone thanks you, and you respond with "it's not a problem" or "it's nothing," do you realize what this means? You're essentially saying that you disagree with their assessment of your contribution. In other words, you are calling them a liar! You're telling them to minimize the impact of what you've done because it's nothing to you. While it may be nothing to you, it could have meant the world to them.

The irony of this is that many of us actually want to hear those words of appreciation or affirmation after we've done something good for someone. It's perfectly natural to expect some appreciation for this. However, some of our responses to those gestures of gratitude contradict that. We pretend as if we're not expecting it. How do I know? Because I've been there before! I've been guilty of this.

Many moons ago, while I was still in college during my undergraduate studies, I would, on occasion, help some of my classmates with homework. One day, after helping Bob (that's not his real name), he just got up and left. He did not say anything to me! Not even a little "thank you" came from him. It's probably because that's not the first time I've helped him with homework. Maybe he thought some of his prior "thanks" counted towards this latest help, but I did not like it.

Instead of confronting him, I cowardly complained to another classmate, Tom (also not his real name), about *ungrateful Bob*. Tom couldn't keep his mouth shut, so he blabbed it to Bob. To his credit, Bob came back to me, apologized and gave the expected "Thank you for helping me." What do you think my response was?

"Oh, it's nothing. Don't mention it!"

What a hypocrite I was! When I did not get the thanks, I pouted. And when I eventually did, I said it was nothing. This is hypocrisy at the highest level! There may be a little of that hypocrisy in you also. So, instead of saying it's nothing, maybe you can simply respond with "You're welcome!" Or you can adopt the response taught to thousands of Chick-fil-A associates: "My Pleasure!" That way, you receive their appreciation with humility. In so doing, you validate their declaration that you've done something positive for them to warrant their thanks.

No Thanks?

My college experience with ungrateful Bob is an example of how one can feel when a good deed goes unacknowledged. No, I'm not talking about my hypocrisy when he returned later to thank me. I'm referring to the feelings that accompany not being appreciated for something specific someone has done. These are feelings that many of us share.

American psychologist and philosopher, William James said, "The deepest principle of human nature is a craving to be appreciated." It doesn't matter how great or small the deed is, the knowledge that what you've done is recognized and appreciated makes the effort worth it. It seems to fulfill a basic human need for significance. So, when an expected gratitude is not delivered, it can lead to feelings of being taken for granted or taken advantage of. With appreciation, however, many positive benefits follow.

For example, all kinds of research have shown that employees who feel more appreciated by their employers tend to be loyal and more productive than those who are not. The result is increased levels of job satisfaction and engagement. On the other hand, not being appreciated is one of the major reasons people leave their employers and look for opportunities elsewhere.

While this is true in the workplace, it is equally valid in personal relationships. Every person that I asked the question about this responded in very emphatic terms about the importance of being appreciated. Here are some of their comments when I asked how they felt when their gracious deed was neither acknowledged nor appreciated:

> "I really got upset. I felt betrayed."[26]

> "It makes me feel hurt. I can become unwilling to want to repeat the situation."[27]

> "I felt invisible, like what I did was completely unseen and unimportant."[28]

> "I always feel bad if the help I rendered was taken for granted."[29]

> "It makes me hesitant to do something for that person again."[30]

> "I felt uncomfortable."[31]

> "I conclude that the person is not worth sacrificing for."[32]

If you're the one on the receiving end of the good deed, it's unlikely that you want the person to feel any of these about you. Yet it happens. When I asked why people had these feelings, their reasons revealed more:

"I feel it's only natural that if I have put forth some effort, that there should be at least some reciprocal acknowledgement."

"The appreciation goes a long way in motivating and encouraging me to do more."

"When you don't hear back, you wonder if it was successful or not. Did I do a good job? Should I have done more?"[33]

"I may begin to think I did not do it the right way."

Over time, with repeated episodes of ingratitude, these feelings and our reasons for having them can eventually lead to negativity, bitterness and resentment. The consequences of these can be devastating. It could lead an employee to seek employment somewhere else. It could lead to a strained relationship between parent and child. It could also lead to a spouse filing for divorce.

You may be wondering why some people may not show appreciation for something done for them. There is a myriad of reasons for this. The most incriminating of these is simply a lack of humility. Proud people don't say thanks. That's because of their high view of their own importance. They feel entitled to whatever you've done for them. You may have gone out of your way to do those things for them, but that's irrelevant. They're too important – more important than you – for them to say thanks to you. Also, there are times when the proud looks at what you've done for them, and they think it doesn't meet their level of importance. They think what you've done doesn't rise to their self-placed level of awesomeness. Your good act belittles them! For most people however, a lack of humility may not be the reason for not showing appreciation.

Some folks are just uncomfortable. I've seen people with such high levels of social anxiety that they have difficulties communicating their gratitude. They hesitate to respond. Because they're not sure of what to say, they say nothing, and you're left to wonder what's going on with them.

Gracious Receptions

Then there are those who are just preoccupied or distracted. Depending on the situation, they may not be immediately aware of what you've done for them because they have other concerns at the moment. Also, some may not realize the amount of effort involved in what you've done. For example, they could think that your agreeing to move a meeting time because of a conflict they have is an easy thing because you're already free at that time. They may not realize the amount of time and persuasion that it took you to make all those phone calls to convince others to reschedule your appointments with them in order to free up that time slot.

Furthermore, research done by eight behavioral scientists, whose results were published in the journal, *Royal Society Open Science*, shows that cultural influences may play a part in how people from different parts of the world show gratitude. These researchers studied more than a thousand casual conversations between people who knew each other well, such as friends and family. These conversations cut across eight languages and multiple cultures in Australia, South America, Western Europe, Africa, Asia, and Eastern Europe. Their findings reveal that in many cases, linguistic traditions are responsible for how people respond when they receive help. They discovered that across cultures, close-knit groups of people take it for granted that people will cooperate with each other, to the point that saying thanks is no longer needed or expected. In their findings, they reported that "in informal everyday interaction across the world, the general norm is to tacitly acknowledge another's cooperative behavior without explicitly saying 'thank you,' but by simply continuing with one's activities, relying on a shared understanding of the good, service or support received as part of a system of social rights and duties governing mutual assistance and collaboration."[34] One of the researchers, Nick Enfield further said that, "in everyday interaction, cooperation is the rule: social life thrives because it's in our nature to ask for help and pay back in kind, rather than just in words."[35] So, expressing gratitude verbally would not be expected in these situations.

Another idea that the researchers proposed as a result of their study is that saying thanks is reserved for when requests go beyond the normal call of duty. I think this specific type cuts across cultures. There are those who may think that for some deeds, saying thanks is unnecessary. They think it's needless because what you did is your responsibility to begin with. "Who thanks people for what they're supposed to be doing?" they ask. While many who espouse this may not consciously ask this question, it may have something to do with how some of us are wired.

I've mentioned before that my natural tendency is to shy away from recognition. I believe that this same inclination makes me feel uneasy when someone thanks me for what I think is my duty. For example, as a husband and a father, I believe it's my responsibility to take care of the needs of my wife and my children. As far as I'm concerned, it's part of the job description. That's what is expected of me. For example, I think it would be odd for one of my children to thank me for putting food on the table or providing a roof over their head, especially during their growing years. I'm not saying it's wrong to thank someone this way. All I'm saying is that for *me*, it would sound weird because those are part of my primary responsibilities. On some occasions, my wife has come to me to say, "Thank you so much for taking care of us and our needs." Each time I've heard that, it makes my stomach churn. I feel awkward and uncomfortable because to me, that's what I'm supposed to do. Because of my uneasiness, I want to shout, "Leave me alone, woman!" But I know better than to do that, so I keep quiet and suffer in silence! Taking a cue from what proper responses look like, what I should have said was, "My pleasure!"

> *The deepest principle of human nature is a craving to be appreciated.*
> William James

As a result of my tendency to shy away from receiving this kind of gratitude, I've discovered that I also have a predisposition toward not giving them. This is true for most of us. How we respond to a particular situation tends to determine how we naturally expect others to respond to the same situation. What we fail to realize is that their nature and personality are different from ours. As a result, they will most likely respond to that situation in a manner that's completely different from ours. If care is not taken, we may get angry at them for not approaching things the same way we would, and it would be for nothing because what we're effectively saying is that we want them to be who they are not. Once you begin to realize that each of us is different from any other person, you can allow them to be who they are, instead of trying to make them conform to your mold.

I want to be very careful here and say that I'm not talking about foundational principles and guidelines upon which a decent, functional society is founded. I'm speaking about style and approach here, especially when these do not violate those foundational principles.

As for my tendency to withhold gratitude from people in the situation I described above, it's an unconscious thing. I just never thought it was necessary because that's what they're supposed to do anyway. I'm not willfully saying I'm not thanking them; it just doesn't cross my mind that I need to. To me, that's what they're expected to do. And that's because if the shoe were on the other foot, my thoughts would be that it's what I'm supposed to do.

I've also found out that this has huge consequences in the workplace. As noted earlier, employees who feel more appreciated by their employers tend to be more loyal and more productive than those who are not. Consistently showing appreciation leads to increased levels of job satisfaction and engagement. For those team leaders who, like me, have the propensity to not commend and appreciate their team members because they think, "That's their job; that's what they're being paid to do," your team will perform much better when you learn to consistently applaud and appreciate what they do. This is true even when you think that it is their responsibility anyway. It's a powerful tool to help motivate and inspire your team to deliver more than you expect.

As for those of you who have leaders like this, try to see things from their perspective. They're probably not knowingly withholding appreciation from you. They may not know that you need it, and that may be because they don't need it. So, why not talk to them about it? Let them know that their compliments and words of encouragement, even for the mundane things that you do every day, is a source of motivation for you. Help them understand how important this is to you. As you do this, you will build bridges to relationships that may last a lifetime.

What You Get
Whether it's how we receive unwanted feedback or the way we respond to positive things others have done for us, the goal should be not to allow our ego to get in the way. When we receive these with humility, it fosters connection with others. It improves our relationship with them.

Receiving feedback with humility can lead to success in both personal and professional relationships. In the workplace, you're seen as coachable and teachable when you have a track record of receiving critical feedback with positive attitude. This can help your career get on the right track. With friends and family, you're easy to talk to because they know you won't bite their heads off when they tell you something you don't want to hear. They will want to be around you.

The same goes for the way you receive thanks, accept help or handle praise. As you continue to do these in ways that shows humility, relationships get better and trust is built.

What You Can Do
Consider doing the following to start showing humility and to become more gracious in receiving both praise and critical feedback:

1. Consider constructive feedback as a gift from those giving them to you. To take away the sting, begin to ask for them, ensure that you really mean it and thank those who have the courage to give you the feedback.

2. Instead of saying, *"No, thank you"* when people offer to help you, learn to be gracious in accepting help, especially when you desperately need it.

3. Seek help when it's evident you need it. Stop thinking you can fix your problems on your own, especially when you have tried many times and failed. Asking for help doesn't make you less than you are. It

Gracious Receptions

enriches you and helps you develop humility.

4. Accepting compliments and commendations from others is a sign of humility. Learn to receive these gracefully.

5. Understand that you did not earn your natural talents; they're given. Begin making efforts to not boast about your accomplishments. Let others do the boasting for you.

EPILOGUE

For most of this book, my intention has been to open your eyes to the immense opportunity that developing humility brings to you and your success in life. It can take you to the highest level that you aspire to, in both your professional career and personal endeavors. It will also keep you at that level as long as you continue to embrace it, learn its lessons and use it to grow.

I'm aware that there are some who may get to high levels of leadership even though they lack aspects of humility in the ways I've described here. This usually happens when the culture or the environment in which such people were able to rise, is one that did not value humility. The good news is that such situations are shrinking by the day, as many have become more aware of the power of being humble to success. For those who may have ascended in these environments, their lack of humility will either ensure that they don't enjoy their success for long, or it will result in a spectacular fall from grace to grass. Even the environment that conspired to place them on a pedestal will eventually realize that such people are not suited for leadership positions. The pride in them will ultimately show up in how they make leadership decisions or in the quality of the decisions they make. This is especially true when they're under pressure and have to navigate difficult circumstances that are beyond their control.

Adversity is a great revealer of character. The decisions we make during difficult situations show the world who we are. When someone makes leadership decisions, they're not the only one impacted by those decisions. This is true whether the decision is made in a domestic context, such as in a family, in business, or with public policy. Within a family, lives can be changed and relationships permanently damaged. In business, the careers of those being led and the longevity of the organization could be affected. With public policy, lives and livelihoods can be irredeemably lost. Nothing brings this to mind more than the recent examples of events that happened on a global scale in the year 2020.

I began to put the finishing touches on this book during the COVID-19 pandemic that engulfed the world at the beginning of that year. As the manner in which different leaders around the world handled the Coronavirus situation unfolded, it was easy for me to see how humility affected how some of them made crucial decisions. The impacts of those decisions are also easily apparent. There were so many examples of how leaders across the globe responded to the pandemic, from which I could pick. However, I will focus on a couple of them that are closer to home for me, to illustrate how the lack of humility, especially in public policy leadership, can lead to disastrous consequences.

I will be comparing the approaches taken by two of the state governors in the United States. In order to protect both of them, I will neither mention their names nor the names of their states. For easy reference, I'll simply refer to them as Governor Kyle and Governor Marcus, and their states as the State of Kyle and the State of Marcus respectively.

A Tale of Two Governors

Allow me to first provide some background information. On January 21, 2020, the United States confirmed its first case of COVID-19 in the State of Washington.[1] Eight days later, U.S. and Japan were the first countries to evacuate their citizens from Wuhan, China, the epicenter of the outbreak. About a month after that (on February 25th), the United States Centers for Disease Control and Prevention (CDC) warned all Americans that the virus was very likely to spread into the country and that people should prepare. On the same day, U.S. senators received a classified briefing on the federal government's Coronavirus response. Soon, the first COVID-19 death in the U.S. was reported on February 29th, the same day that Washington State declared a state of emergency. By March 8th, eight states in the country had declared a state of emergency.[2] With this, it's reasonable to expect that other states would perhaps begin to pay attention, especially if that state

Adversity is a great revealer of character.

Epilogue

happened to have large metropolitan areas with huge populations. But it did not seem as if Governor Kyle was paying attention, even though his state was home to a metro area that was in the top ten (in terms of population) in the country.

As of March 13, sixteen states had announced that schools would be closing in an attempt to stem the rise in Coronavirus cases. On this same date, the U.S. President declared a state of national emergency. The very next day, on March 14th, Governor Kyle finally declared a state of emergency for his state. In case you just missed it, that move came only after a national state of emergency had already been declared, and after every other state, with the exception of West Virginia had reported Coronavirus cases. All of these provided a backdrop for how Governor Kyle provided leadership for the citizens of his state during the pandemic.

Despite the emergency declaration by Kyle, a statewide shutdown was not mandated until early April. It took a few weeks after other states had taken initial precautions by shutting down before Governor Kyle finally decided it was a good idea to do so. Meanwhile, his state's Coronavirus cases were surging. Why would he do this? Why did he wait until things got from bad to worse before taking action? Was he waiting for more information? Granted that not a lot was known about this new virus at the time, but it was obvious to many leaders that inaction was not the way to go.

From the way I saw it, Kyle's hesitation to do what was needed has to do with a lack of humility. Here's my reason for this – Governor Kyle apparently believed he knew better than the other states who took early initial precautions. Many of these states were smaller than his. Even when medical and public health experts were saying there were still a lot of unknowns about the virus, and recommended the actions taken by the other states, Governor Kyle thought he was more aware of the situation; much more than what the experts were saying. His personal opinions weighed heavier than those of the professionals. He felt he knew more than the experts, so he did not listen to them. He had a high view of his own importance.

When Kyle eventually decided to shut down the state, he couldn't own up to his previous mistakes about delaying the shutdown unnecessarily. Instead, he announced that he had decided to shut down because he had just learned something "game-changing" about the virus. He claimed he had just learned – within the past twenty-four hours of his announcement – that the virus could be transmitted to others before the infected person develops symptoms. American late-night comics had a field day with this because for several weeks, the fact that an infected person without symptoms could transmit the virus to others had been a widely-accepted belief. In fact, this was one of the major reasons many states around the country locked down much earlier. But Kyle couldn't admit to his mistakes because his pride would not allow him to. It takes humility to recognize and own up to mistakes. He could not admit to his mistakes because his view of his own importance was too high for him to do so.

What's more baffling to many is that despite being one of the last states to shut down, Governor Kyle decided his state would be among the first in the nation to reopen. He brought back businesses (gyms, hair salons, nail salons, movie theaters and restaurants) that were known to help the virus' spread.[3] Guidelines from the CDC and the federal government task force on the pandemic required that for states to reopen, new infections should have been on the decrease for at least fourteen consecutive days.[4] This was not the situation in the State of Kyle when he decided to reopen the state. His shutdown lasted less than one month as he abruptly reversed course and even overruled the restrictions put in place by mayors in the state.

His orders shocked people across the country. Both scientists and high-ranking officials from his state (some of whom belonged to the same political party as him) condemned the reopening. What this showed was that his decision to reopen was a unilateral one. It was done without consultation with his own team and other state leaders. He did not need to consult with anyone since he knew the best course to take – he knew it all! His action even drew a public rebuke from the President, who was reported to have initially approved his reopening plans before distancing himself after the backlash came furiously.

Epilogue

When Governor Kyle decided to reopen bars in June 2020, the consequences were easily predictable: new Coronavirus case counts jumped back up. A lot more people in the state became sick from the virus, which overwhelmed medical officials and facilities. The death rate also increased. Many died because their governor was a know-it-all, who couldn't or simply wouldn't ask for advice from health officials and other states about what was working and what was not.

Furthermore, after the wearing of face masks had been publicly promoted by experts as effective in reducing the spread of the virus, Kyle repeatedly refused to require masks in his state. In fact, the state's pandemic emergency order he wrote was written with an explicit restriction to prevent local leaders within the state from implementing their own mask rules. Consequently, he filed a lawsuit against the mayor of the largest city in his state when she mandated the wearing of face masks and planned to roll back the city's reopening. When the mayor fought back, he tried to stop her from issuing statements and speaking to the press.[5] This may seem completely made-up if you're just becoming aware of this now, but it's true. Such an action sounds unreasonable to most people who know a thing or two about leadership. But the proud doesn't live in the realm of reason. The proud person lives in his own self-made world. He is the king of that world, and he rules it with an iron fist! Nobody else matters – not even the subjects over whom he is king. Whether they like it or not, they must comply.

What Kyle seemed to have forgotten was that he's not a king, even though he had tried to rule like one. As an elected leader of his state, he can easily be voted out. With his bungling of the pandemic, his approval rating as of early August 2020 had dropped by sixteen percentage points from where it was at the beginning of that year.[6] Eventually, with his political future seemingly fading away, he backtracked. In mid-August, he withdrew his lawsuit against the mayor and signed another executive order that empowered many cities and counties to impose face covering requirements to

The proud doesn't live in the realm of reason. The proud person lives in his own self-made world.

combat the coronavirus. His political opponents saw the reversal simply as an attempt to save face[7], because cities in the state already had a face mask mandate in place despite his former strong objections.

I think he changed course because his political fortunes were dwindling. He still had more than two years before his reelection would come up in November 2022. It would be interesting to see if he's able to turn things around before then in order to get re-elected, or if he will be a one-term governor. As of this moment, my hope is that he would realize that the path he was on would not help his re-election efforts. Following that realization should be an admission that he was wrong, but I'm not holding my breath for that. He would have to change his approach and tactics, consult with leaders within his state and work with them for the betterment of his people.

In a poll released by *The Washington Post*, respondents were asked whether they approved of the job their state governor was doing in dealing with the coronavirus pandemic. Out of the twelve states with sample sizes large enough to break down the results, eleven states had constituents approving the job their state governors had done.[8] It should come as no surprise that Governor Kyle was the lone exception. In that same poll, the governor of the State of Marcus led the pack with the highest percentage of his people approving his leadership during the pandemic. What did he do differently?

Governor Marcus took an aggressive and early response to the pandemic. Unlike the State of Kyle, it also did not rush its reopening. Marcus used scientific data to drive his decision to shut down early and to ensure a measured reopening. His daily briefings on the pandemic were done alongside Dr. Emily (not her real name), the State's director of public health. With their daily news conferences, they both presented a united leadership front to their citizens.

Instead of fighting with the leaders in his State, Governor Marcus worked with them. Rather than taking those who disagreed with him to court, he chose to collaborate with them. The result was a much lower percentage of positive cases when

Epilogue

compared with the State of Kyle. Experts believed this led to many lives being saved in the state.

Texas A&M School of Public Health professor Gerard Carrino said the State of Marcus was "doing well so far because leaders successfully balanced the health, economics, and politics of the state."[9] He further stated, "We're learning now from states that shut down late and opened up early that it can't all be about economics because people get sick and people die." At the time he made these statements, the states that prioritized the economy were grappling with the consequences. The State of Kyle was one of them.

To be clear, it wasn't as if Governor Marcus and Dr. Emily did not have any detractors within their state. Oh yes, they did! Some citizens of their state picketed the statehouse and some even protested in front of Dr. Emily's house because they were unhappy with the closures and the resulting economic downturn. Despite that, Marcus remained overwhelmingly popular with the residents of his state. That's because he communicated daily in plain language that everyone could understand using objective and science-based facts. He did not allow politics, pressure, or his own personal preferences to dictate his response.

After all, the reality of COVID-19 would not respond to politics or personal opinions, no matter how good those may seem to the people who wanted to keep the economy open. In the face of opposition, I thought Governor Marcus showed exceptional humility in his handling of the Coronavirus pandemic in his state. Because of that, many of his citizens were spared from the devastating effects of the disease. At least, this was the situation as of June 2020. With the Coronavirus pandemic still raging at the time of this writing, only hindsight will reveal if these governors will be vindicated or incriminated by the type of leadership they provided.

Even though the COVID-19 pandemic was experienced on a global scale, it became a very divisive issue in the United States. Political opponents seized it as an opportunity to demonize those on the other side of the aisle. Given the charged partisan environment in America at the time this book is being released, it is conceivable that some may see my portrayal of these two governors through political lenses.

However, it is not my intention to inject politics into these examples. In fact, I have tried throughout the entire text of this book to ensure that what I communicated had not been tainted by politics. That was a deliberate effort on my part. I may not have been completely successful with it, but that was my goal. This was also the reason I ensured that the two governors used as examples belonged to the same political party. If they were not, it's possible that someone could read beyond the surface and inject partisanship into it. Despite that, it's still likely that a few people would see these illustrations as political. This is especially possible if they agree with the politics of Governor Kyle or disagree with that of Governor Marcus. I think the key problem is that we have allowed our politics to taint the way we experience life with others. We no longer see things clearly as they really are. We continue to allow our biases and prejudices to discolor what we see. Truth seems to have fallen in our streets.

It is unfortunate that we can no longer have a public discourse, and disagree on principles without casting aspersions on one another. In this type of environment, we're quick to accuse those who are supposed to be our friends and family as belonging to the enemy's camp. Within one year of the appearance of COVID-19, I have heard of families torn apart, churches split, and members of the same community at odds with one another. We have given people we supposedly "know" through television and social media unfettered access into our homes to cause division. We have ceded control of some of our most-prized relationships to those who have no idea how important,

We no longer see things clearly as they really are. Truth seems to have fallen in our streets.

priceless and precious those relationships are to us. We have allowed these people to drive a wedge between us and those we love most dearly. My friends, this should not be the case.

So, if you happen to see the examples of these governors through the eyes of politics, I'm going to ask you to think through why this is the case for you. Ponder what beliefs in you make you

Epilogue

see them this way, and reflect on the consequences these may be having on your relationships with others. I have not seen these examples through political lenses; and I definitely do not think I have portrayed them that way. My intention has been to highlight how having humility or the lack of it can affect each one of us, especially those in leadership positions of high visibility – whether that's in politics or in business. While the stakes are high for us in our individual spheres of influence, it is higher for them in their leadership roles.

The fact remains that the path to the top, and staying there is laced with humility. In his book, *Derailed*, Tim Irwin profiled six leaders whose careers went off the tracks. He said that arrogance is the mother of all derailers. Irwin wrote, "While a failure of character can manifest itself in many ways, the most foundational and most self-destructive is arrogance. Just as humility seems to be at the epicenter of leadership effectiveness, arrogance is commonly at the root of a leader's undoing . . . and ours."[10] Even if you're not currently occupying a corporate leadership or a visibly political leadership position, you need humility to succeed in anything you do. You need it to build and enjoy loving relationships with those who are important to you.

Contrary to what many believe, people who are humble are often fearless. They're able to act on their convictions in the face of strong opposition. But they do it in a manner that is neither threatening nor offensive to others. They do not seek to impress other people. They make decisions using sound, fact-based reasoning, but they also consider people's feelings. They don't allow insecurity or prejudice to cloud their judgement. They listen eagerly and welcome candid differences in opinion. They encourage critics, and do not get crushed by their criticisms. They often treat all people with respect. Consequently, they engender and provoke loyalty within their spheres of influence. Many of us *You need humility to succeed in anything you do.* want to work with humble people. We like working for them, and enjoy having them work for us. We desire to have them as colleagues, friends, spouses, and family members. But most importantly, we should want to become humble ourselves.

205

ΝΟΤΗΙΝG ΗΙGHER

The good news is that you and I have the means and the power within us to do something about it. We can learn to be humble. My hope is that through the pages of this book, you've been able to see that this is possible. I also hope that I've been able to spark in you the flame that will motivate you to sincerely desire to live a life of ongoing humility. That desire must lead to action. If it doesn't, you're just deceiving yourself.

Your performance gap lies in the difference between what you know and what you do. What you know must translate into what you do for you to attract success. You now know that you must learn to descend in order to soar. Your next move should be to put the practical steps in this book into action. Therein lies your success. There's simply no other way to be happy and achieve greatness in this life.

There's really nothing higher.

NOTES & REFERENCES

Prologue

1. Mel Kaup; Humility survey comments, October 13, 2017; 8:50 pm.

2. Kimberly Powers; Humility survey comments, October 13, 2017; 10:43 pm.

3. Temitope Olalude; Humility survey comments, October 14, 2017; 10:40 am.

4. Mary Birchenough; Humility survey comments, October 14, 2017; 4:49 pm.

5. Vivien Obieke; Humility survey comments, October 16, 2017; 10:38 am.

6. Tony Schwartz, *Finding Strength in Humility*; Dealbook – New York Times blog; https://dealbook.nytimes.com/2013/11/15/finding-strength-in-humility/ ; November 15, 2013

7. Bob McCoy; Humility survey comments, October 13, 2017; 9:10 pm.

Chapter 1

1. Proverbs 18:16; New King James Version of the Holy Bible.

2. Gary Hoyt; Humility interview. October 3, 2017.

3. Richard James; Humility survey comments, October 14, 2017; 7:04 am.

4. Walter Hooker; Humility interview. December 13, 2017.

5. Oluremi Odediran; Humility survey comments, October 20, 2017; 3:12 pm.

6. Kevin Barrett; Humility survey comments, October 13, 2017; 8:05 pm.

7. Nair Hernandez; Humility survey comments, October 13, 2017; 9:04 pm.

8. Melba Hooker; Humility survey comments, October 13, 2017; 9:22 pm.

Chapter 2

1. Mario Livio; *"Why Do We Ask Why?"*; Psychology Today, June 23, 2017; https://www.psychologytoday.com/blog/why/201706/why-do-we-ask-why

2. Walter Hooker; Humility interview. December 13, 2017.

3. Mary Coleman; Humility survey comments, October 13, 2017; 8:48 pm.

4. Kimberly Powers; Humility survey comments, October 13, 2017; 10:43 pm.

5. Deb Joy; Humility survey comments, October 14, 2017; 4:27 am.

6. Brenda Kucera; Humility survey comments, October 21, 2017; 6:08 am.

7. Bob McCoy; Humility survey comments, October 21, 2017; 9:40 am.

8. Deborah Joy; Humility survey comments, October 22, 2017; 4:39 am.

9. Katherine Fox; Humility survey comments, October 22, 2017; 3:40 pm.

10. Kimberly Powers; Humility survey comments, October 27, 2017; 9:48 pm.

11. Paul Faronbi; Humility survey comments, October 25, 2017; 4:20 am.

12. Kevin Barrett; Humility survey comments, October 28,

2017; 5:57 pm.

13. Bob McCoy; Humility survey comments, October 28, 2017; 7:28 pm.

14. Adekunle Ayoade; Humility survey comments, October 29, 2017; 12:25 pm.

15. Mary Birchenough; Humility survey comments, October 29, 2017; 4:42 pm.

16. Jacqueline Schnider; Humility survey comments, October 30, 2017; 1:16 pm.

17. Olu-Samuel Akintobi; Humility survey comments, November 2, 2017; 9:19 pm.

18. Richard James; Humility survey comments, November 2, 2017; 2:29 pm.

19. Femi Awodele; Humility interview. October 5, 2017.

20. Bradley P. Owens, Michael D. Johnson and Terence R. Mitchell, *"Expressed Humility in Organizations: Implications for Performance, Teams, and Leadership"*; Organization Science, Vol. 24, No. 5, Sept – Oct 2013, Pages 1517 – 1538

21. Rob Nielsen, Jennifer A. Marrone, and Holly S. Slay, *"A New Look at Humility: Exploring the Humility Concept and Its Role in Socialized Charismatic Leadership"*; Journal of Leadership and Organizational Studies, Nov. 24, 2009.

Additional source with no notation in text:

Olumuyiwa Olofinjana; Humility survey comments, October 30, 2017; 3:25 pm.

Chapter 3

1. Judge Judy; *"Judge Judy Puts the Smack Down on Welfare Mother"*; https://www.youtube.com/watch?v=2K1bhRX7tN8; January 9, 2015.

2. Richard James; Humility survey comments, January 19, 2018; 10:12 pm.

3. Kimberly Powers; Humility survey comments, January 12, 2018; 9:28 pm.

4. Katherine Fox; Humility survey comments, February 5, 2018; 1:15 pm.

5. Andy Stanley, *"Enemies of the Heart: Breaking Free from the Four Emotions that Control You"*; Crown Publishing Group, 2011.

6. Femi Awodele; Humility interview. October 5, 2017.

7. William H. Willimon and Thomas H. Naylor, *"The Abandoned Generation: Rethinking Higher Education"*; Wm. B. Eerdmans Publishing Co., July 1995, Pages 38-39.

8. The Giving Pledge; https://givingpledge.org/About.aspx

9. Melba Hooker; Humility survey comments, January 5, 2018; 8:25 pm.

10. Nair Hernandez; Humility survey comments, January 5, 2018; 10:22 pm.

11. Mary Coleman; Humility survey comments, January 6, 2018; 2:22 pm.

12. Amit Amin, *"The Science of Gratitude: More Benefits Than Expected"*; http://happierhuman.com/the-science-of-gratitude;

13. Gary Hoyt; Humility interview. October 3, 2017.

14. Walter Hooker; Humility interview. December 13, 2017.

Additional source with no notation in text:

Melba Hooker; Humility survey comments, January 20, 2018; 12:17 pm.

Chapter 4

1. Susan Krauss Whitbourne. *"Bragging, When Is It OK*

and When Is It Not OK?"
https://www.psychologytoday.com/blog/fulfillment-any-age/201207/bragging-when-is-it-ok-and-when-is-it-not-ok, July 2012.

2. Banke Adebowale; Humility survey comments, November 20, 2017; 12:20 pm.

3. Yemmy Ojo; Humility survey comments, November 17, 2017; 10:43 pm.

4. Melba Hooker; Humility survey comments, November 17, 2017; 11:50 pm.

5. Bob McCoy; Humility survey comments, November 18, 2017; 4:25 am.

6. Nair Hernandez; Humility survey comments, November 18, 2017; 6:09 am.

7. Irene Scopelliti, George Loewenstein, Joachim Vosgerau. *You Call It "Self-Exuberance"; I Call It "Bragging" – Miscalibrated Predictions of Emotional Responses to Self-Promotion*; Psychological Science, Volume 26, Issue 6; June 1, 2015

8. Millon, Theodore (2003). *Handbook of Psychology, Personality and Social Psychology*. John Wiley & Sons. p. 337. ISBN 9780471384045.

9. Associated Press. *"Ex-Viagra salesman fired for boastful book"*; http://www.nbcnews.com/id/7320442/ns/business-us_business/t/ex-viagra-salesman-fired-boastful-book#.WSMQ52jyvIU; NBCNews.com; March 2005.

10. *Phobia List – The Ultimate List of Phobias and Fears*; http://www.fearof.net

11. César Hernandez; Humility survey comments, November 14, 2017; 6:22 pm.

12. Jacquie Schnider; Humility survey comments, November 14, 2017; 10:02 am.

13. Nair Hernandez; Humility survey comments, November 12, 2017; 7:44 am.

14. Olu-Samuel Akintobi; Humility survey comments, November 12, 2017; 5:04 am.

15. Richard James; Humility survey comments, November 11, 2017; 10:01 pm.

16. Kevin Barrett; Humility survey comments, November 11, 2017; 2:06 pm.

17. Mary Birchenough; Humility survey comments, November 13, 2017; 7:16 pm.

Additional sources with no notation in text:

Adekunle Ayoade; Humility survey comments, November 14, 2017; 2:57 pm.

Katherine Fox; Humility survey comments, November 27, 2017; 9:41 am.

Brenda Kucera; Humility survey comments, November 13, 2017; 11:34 am.

Jinad-Akande Ismaila Kolawole; Humility survey comments, November 12, 2017; 1:18 pm.

Bob McCoy; Humility survey comments, November 11, 2017; 9:18 am.

Walter Hooker; Humility interview. December 13, 2017.

Chapter 5

1. Oluremi Odediran; Humility survey comments, February 2, 2018; 11:06 am.

2. Rebecca Fegan; Humility survey comments, January 27, 2018; 10:52 pm.

3. Olu-Samuel Akintobi; Humility survey comments, February 3, 2018; 3:47 am.

4. Kevin Barrett; Humility survey comments, February 3, 2018; 6:53 am.

Notes & References

5. Rebecca Fegan; Humility survey comments, February 3, 2018; 9:09 am.

6. Bob McCoy; Humility survey comments, February 3, 2018; 11:34 am.

7. Kimberly Powers; Humility survey comments, February 3, 2018; 8:55 pm.

8. Jacquie Schnider; Humility survey comments, February 6, 2018; 8:54 am.

9. Katherine Fox; Humility survey comments, February 12, 2018; 8:59 pm.

10. Jinad-Akande Ismaila Kolawole; Humility survey comments, February 9, 2018; 2:40 pm.

11. Nair Hernandez; Humility survey comments, February 3, 2018; 3:08 pm.

12. Oluremi Odediran; Humility survey comments, February 6, 2018; 10:04 am.

13. Arthur Jones; *In High School Stephen Miller Complained About Picking up His Own Trash*; http://ir.net/news/politics/126599/high-school-stephen-miller-complained-picking-trash/ August 6, 2017.

14. Greenleaf, Robert K. *"The Power of Servant-Leadership: Essays"* Berrett-Koehler Publishers; 1 edition – September 1998. Page 123.

15. Peterson, Matt. *"A True Story to Share on Servant Leadership and Talent Development"*; Aethos Consulting Group, https://www.aethoscg.com/aethos_insights/a-true-story-to-share-on-servant-leadership-and-talent-development;

16. Somaiya, Ravi and Kaufman, Leslie. *"If a Story Is Viral, Truth May Be Taking a Beating"* The New York Times, New York Edition. December 10, 2013. Page B1.

17. Bob McCoy; Humility survey comments, January 15, 2018; 3:52 pm.

18. Adekunle Ayoade; Humility survey comments, February 3, 2018; 2:31 pm.

19. Kevin Barrett; Humility survey comments, February 19, 2018; 9:09 am.

20. Kimberly Powers; Humility survey comments, February 19, 2018; 9:23 am.

21. Adekunle Ayoade; Humility survey comments, February21, 2018; 11:00 am.

22. Assad Schuitem; *"The Importance of Respect in Teams"*; http://careandgrowth.com/blog/teamexcellence/2015/11/03/the-importance-of-respect-in-teams; Intent Blog, November 2015.

23. Del Jones, *"CEOs say how you treat a waiter can predict a lot about character"* http://usatoday30.usatoday.com/money/companies/management/2006-04-14-ceos-waiter-rule_x.htm. USA Today. Updated April 17, 2006.

24. Walter Hooker; Humility interview. December 13, 2017.

Chapter 6

1. Richard Bray; *"Deepwater Horizon oil spill: BP gaffes in full"*; https://www.theguardian.com/business/2010/jul/27/deepwater-horizon-oil-spill-bp-gaffes. The Guardian, July 27, 2010.

2. Ibid

3. Ibid

4. Allan Chernoff; *"CNN: Tony Hayward's downfall"*; https://www.youtube.com/watch?v=OeAKemBrgGw; CNN Report, July 27, 2010.

5. Bryan Walsh; *"Oil Spill: Goodbye, Mr. Hayward"*; http://science.time.com/2010/07/25/oil-spill-goodbye-mr-hayward. TIME Magazine, July 25, 2010.

6. Tim Webb; *"BP boss admits job on the line over Gulf oil spill"*; https://www.theguardian.com/business/2010/may/13/bp-boss-admits-mistakes-gulf-oil-spill. The Guardian, May 13, 2010.

7. Jim Whitehurst; *"Be a Leader Who Can Admit Mistakes."* https://hbr.org/2015/06/be-a-leader-who-can-admit-mistakes. Harvard Business Review, June 2, 2015.

8. Rock, David. *"Your Brain at Work"*; HarperBusiness. October 2009. Page 130.

9. Melba Hooker; Humility survey comments, March 3, 2018; 10:09 am.

10. Rebecca Fegan; Humility survey comments, March 3, 2018; 12:29 pm.

11. Jacquie Schnider; Humility survey comments, March 6, 2018; 4:20 pm.

12. Mary Coleman; Humility survey comments, April 16, 2018; 7:57 pm.

13. Olu-Samuel Akintobi; Humility survey comments, March 16, 2018; 11:04 am.

14. Bob McCoy; Humility survey comments, April 15, 2018; 4:03 pm.

15. Katherine Fox; Humility survey comments, March 27, 2018; 10:25 am.

16. Adekunle Ayoade; Humility survey comments, April 19, 2018; 6:45 pm.

17. Jacquie Schnider; Humility survey comments, March 19, 2018; 1:40 pm.

18. César Hernandez; Humility survey comments, April 15, 2018; 8:14 am.

19. Ismaila Kolawole Jinad-Akande; Humility survey comments, April 15, 2018; 10:56 am.

20. Adekunle Ayoade; Humility survey comments, March 19, 2018; 12:47 pm.

21. Paresky, Pamela B.; *"Can You Spot a Know-it-All?"* Psychology Today, May 21, 2015. https://www.psychologytoday.com/blog/happiness-and-the-pursuit-leadership/201505/can-you-spot-know-it-all.

22. Omolara Akinbola; Humility survey comments, April 20, 2018; 3:12 pm.

23. Adekunle Ayoade; Humility survey comments, April 7, 2018; 7:41 pm.

24. Rebecca Fegan; Humility survey comments, April 7, 2018; 7:40 am.

25. Story courtesy of Paul Faronbi.

26. Adekunle Ayoade; Humility survey comments, April 21, 2018; 9:09 pm.

27. Vivien Obieke; Humility survey comments, April 21, 2018; 1:57 am.

28. Melba Hooker; Humility survey comments, May 14, 2018; 9:12 am.

Chapter 7

1. Stein, Steven and Book, Howard; *The EQ Edge: Emotional Intelligence and Your Success*, 3rd Edition. Page 175.

2. César Hernandez; Humility survey comments, May 26, 2018; 4:54 am.

3. Katherine Fox; Humility survey comments, July 23, 2018; 9:47 am.

4. Walter Hooker; Humility interview. December 13, 2017.

5. Femi Awodele; Humility interview. October 5, 2017.

6. Kimberly Powers; Humility survey comments, July 7, 2018; 7:37 pm.

Notes & References

7. Psalms 139:14; The Holy Bible, New Living Translation.

8. Numbers 12; The Holy Bible, English Standard Version.

9. Rebecca Fegan; Humility survey comments, July 4, 2018; 11:11 pm.

10. Raquel Porter; Humility survey comments, June 15, 2018; 9:13 pm.

11. Adekunle Ayoade; Humility survey comments, June 20, 2018; 9:44 pm.

12. Kimberly Powers; Humility survey comments, July 7, 2018; 7:45 pm.

13. Jacquie Schnider; Humility survey comments, July 16, 2018; 11:14 am.

14. Kimberly Powers; Humility survey comments, July 7, 2018; 7:49 pm.

15. Melba Hooker; Humility survey comments, July 6, 2018; 9:79 pm.

16. Rebecca Fegan; Humility survey comments, July 7, 2018; 7:12 am.

17. Nair Hernandez; Humility survey comments, July 24, 2018; 9:02 pm.

18. Kille, David R., Eibach, Richard P., Wood, Joanne V. and Holmes, John G.; *Who can't take a compliment? The role of construal level and self-esteem in accepting positive feedback from close others*; Journal of Experimental Social Psychology, May 2016.

19. Jason Owens; *"Yasiel Puig admits he 'never worked hard' in L.A, vows to up effort in contract year with Reds"*; Yahoo Sports; February 25, 2019; https://sports.yahoo.com/yasiel-puig-admits-he-never-worked-hard-in-la-vows-to-up-effort-in-contract-year-with-reds-012121974.html.

20. Melba Hooker; Humility survey comments, July 13,

2018; 9:12 pm.

21. Vivien Obieke; Humility survey comments, July 18, 2018; 3:17 pm.

22. Bob McCoy; Humility survey comments, July 16, 2018; 8:05 am.

23. Nair Hernandez; Humility survey comments, July 15, 2018; 4:22 pm.

24. Jacquie Schnider; Humility survey comments, July 16, 2018; 11:10 am.

25. Hope Valentine; Humility survey comments, July 16, 2018; 7:08 pm.

26. Rebecca Fegan; Humility survey comments, July 21, 2018; 12:57 am.

27. Bob McCoy; Humility survey comments, July 21, 2018; 3:08 am.

28. Katherine Fox; Humility survey comments, July 23, 2018; 8:52 am.

29. Adekunle Ayoade; Humility survey comments, July 24, 2018; 11:26 am.

30. Jacquie Schnider; Humility survey comments, August 3, 2018; 2:50 pm.

31. Omolara Akinbola; Humility survey comments, August 19, 2018; 9:29 am.

32. Oluremi Odediran; Humility survey comments, August 23, 2018; 12:02 pm.

33. Melba Hooker; Humility survey comments, August 2, 2018; 4:37 pm.

34. Floyd S, Rossi G, Baranova J, Blythe J, Dingemanse M, Kendrick KH, Zinken J, Enfield NJ.; *"Universals and cultural diversity in the expression of gratitude."* Royal Society Open Science; R. Soc. open sci.5: 180391. May 23, 2018. http://dx.doi.org/10.1098/rsos.180391

Notes & References

35. Ian Sample; *"People rarely say thank you when others help them out, scientists say"*; The Guardian, May 22, 2018.

Additional source with no notation in text:

Proverbs 12:1; The Holy Bible, New International Version.

Epilogue

1. Caroline Kantis, Samantha Kiernan, and Jason Socrates Bardi; *"UPDATED: Timeline of the Coronavirus"*; Think Global Health, July 27, 2020. https://www.thinkglobalhealth.org/article/updated-timeline-coronavirus

2. Matthew Impelli; *"What U.S. States Have Declared a State of Emergency Amid Coronavirus Outbreak"*; Newsweek, March 9, 2020. https://www.newsweek.com/what-us-states-have-declared-state-emergency-amid-coronavirus-outbreak-1491299

3. Amanda Mull; *"Georgia's Experiment in Human Sacrifice"*; The Atlantic, April 29, 2020. https://www.theatlantic.com/health/archive/2020/04/why-georgia-reopening-coronavirus-pandemic/610882/

4. Centers for Disease Control and Prevention; *"CDC Activities and Initiatives Supporting the COVID-19 Response and the President's Plan for Opening America Up Again"*; May 2020, Pp 25, 27; https://www.cdc.gov/coronavirus/2019-ncov/downloads/php/CDC-Activities-Initiatives-for-COVID-19-Response.pdf

5. Michael King; *"Bottoms bristles at request for emergency injunction against speaking to press"*; 11Alive, July 19, 2020; https://www.11alive.com/article/news/health/coronavirus/bottoms-bristles-at-request-for-emergency-injunction-

against-speaking-to-press/85-3fba7088-9142-476a-a3bd-7aff677229f2

6. Amanda Mull; *"America's Authoritarian Governor"*; The Atlantic, August 8, 2020; https://www.theatlantic.com/health/archive/2020/08/geor gia-brian-kemp-authoritarian/615010/

7. Greg Bluestein; *"In reversal, Kemp's new order to let some cities impose mask mandates"*; Political Insider Blog, The Atlanta Journal-Constitution, August 14, 2020; https://www.ajc.com/politics/politics-blog/kemps-new-order-to-allow-some-cities-to-impose-mask-mandates/Z64MTLEXMVCEFEHESMUEG3BERI/

8. Chris Cillizza; *"Guess which governor's coronavirus response is the least popular"*; CNN Politics, May 13, 2020; https://www.cnn.com/2020/05/13/politics/brian-kemp-coronavirus-georgia-poll/index.html

9. Mary Kilpatrick; *"How has Ohio avoided a coronavirus spike while other states surge? Experts credit early closings, measured reopenings"*; Cleveland.com, June 19, 2020; https://www.cleveland.com/metro/2020/06/how-has-ohio-avoided-a-coronavirus-spike-experts-credit-early-closings-measured-reopenings.html

10. Tim Irwin; *"Derailed – Five Lessons Learned from Catastrophic Failures of Leadership"*; Thomas Nelson Publishers. 2009.

ABOUT THE AUTHOR

A conference speaker and coach to project managers, STEM[1] professionals and executives, **Sunday Faronbi (Sunny)** has had the unique opportunity to experience different cultures both personally and professionally.

After growing up in Africa and spending the first eight years of his career as an engineer in Nigeria, Sunny relocated to the United States. For most of his engineering and project management career spanning more than 25 years, he executed engineering projects and led teams of professionals in multiple disciplines and across different cultures in different parts of the globe.

An avid traveler, Sunny brings unique perspectives gleaned from real-world experiences. Audiences and readers alike love the practical applications he brings from his insights, including the role that humility plays in building relationships, accelerating careers, and improving personal well-being.

As a keynote speaker and business coach, Sunny frequently taps into his more than three decades of professional experience during his coaching and mentoring sessions, and whenever he speaks at conferences. In addition, he regularly facilitates seminars and workshops on leadership and emotional intelligence topics for companies and professional organization around the world.

For more information on booking Sunny as a speaker for your event or to engage him as a business coach, you can reach him through his website at www.SunnySpeaks.com.

---

[1] STEM - Science, Technology, Engineering and Mathematics

If you have found this book valuable, and you can think of at least one other person who will benefit from its contents, please recommend it to them. Also, consider leaving a review.